I0429436

PRACTICAL GUIDE TO EVENTS PLANNING

HARRIET GRAYSON

Ocean Breeze Press
RI

Practical Guide to Events Planning
Harriet Grayson

Published by Ocean Breeze Press
Rhode Island

Manufactured in United States

Library of Congress Cataloguing-in-Publication Data Grayson, Harriet

PRACTICAL GUIDE TO EVENTS PLANNING/ Harriet Grayson

TABLE OF CONTENTS

Chapter 1 Introduction: Where to Begin

Although it may look effortless, planning special events can be a daunting experience. Making the complex appear like child's play is the handiwork of an experienced events planner whether they work for a non-profit, hotel or resort, college, government, corporation or consulting firm.

This is an exciting and growing field. People are attracted to it because it implies flair and creativity. And it does. But it also requires an organized mind and a predilection for details. Long days and endless nights is part of the job description. And fun. Events planners do have fun and the career choices are so varied.

Career Choices

According to the US Department of Labor, more than 50,000 people are employed as *meeting and convention planners*, which is the formal, federal occupational designation. Of these, more than a quarter (27%) work for non-profits; almost a fifth work (17%) in the hotel industry; 8 percent work for educational services including colleges and universities, and private schools. Three percent work for government including federal, state and local while 6 percent are self-employed as events planning consultants. The remaining workers are employed by trade show organizing firms or for corporations as events planners.

1

Event planning is big business. During flush times, it can translate into $500 billion annually spent by various types of organizations. Even in tight times, individuals, corporations, small businesses, non-profits spend money to raise awareness, celebrate, educate, honor or market and advertise. In recent years, as non-profits have downsized staff because of falling revenues and smaller donations, special events planning has moved from an in-house function to outside events planning firms. Laid-off events planners and other development staff have created new businesses as consultants often making as a first client a former employer.

Economic times can foster changes in the industry. When companies are prospering there is more to spend. Elaborate events become the norm. During tight economic times the traditional holiday party must be created on a shoe string budget.

Industries that require licensure and certification are always in need of educational conferences regardless of the economic temperature. The health care industry is an excellent example. It requires conferences and meetings regardless of the economy. Another group that increasingly finds the need to receive continuing education credits is educational professions: teachers, school administrators, school psychologists and social workers.

What activities define an event planner?

One of the most exciting aspects of the job is that events planners are expected to perform a wide number and range of tasks. The starting point is articulating the purpose or goal of any event. The events planner may not define that goal but they are responsible for translating the goal into a successful and positively memorable occasion. It is often the events planner who selects the venue, speakers, entertainment, food, and possibly the date.

The events planner becomes the bicycle's wheel hub, all actions emanate from them. Event participants depend upon them for decisions dealing with lodging, exhibit space, meals, type and number, telecommunications, audio-visual equipment and transportation. They also must juggle vendors and become conversant in the details of contract legalese, masters of indisputable accounting practices to balance budgets and spatial designers in selecting just the right look of the event. The events planner is a transportation planner responsible for a location close to public transportation or accessible by major highways. The compliments may be few but there is no shortage of critics. Events planners often work with a fickle audience. A rising current of criticism can lead to the hasty departure of the events planner from the organization.

Fundraising is the major difference between the for-profit & non-profit worlds

The major difference between a special events planner for a non-profit versus working for business is that special events are often the financial life blood of a non-profit. This adds stress to an already inherently stressful career. Not all special events for non-profits are fundraising activities. There are special events designed to increase awareness of an issue or awareness of the organization. An example of such an event is a ribbon-cutting where politicians are invited as well as community leaders.

Those working for companies in the marketing and sales departments or in special travel departments are not directly involved with fundraising. However, companies either through their Charitable Giving offices, sometimes Human Resources, or Public or

Community Affairs will often become sponsors of non-profit fundraising activities. They will buy tables at a non-profit's gala, support a walkathon, and provide prizes at a golf tournament. Those working in the hotel/resort industry will often be called upon to assist non-profits in their fundraising activities since many non-profits use hotels and resorts as venues.

Educational Requirements

In today's rapidly changing world of meetings and events, the expectation is that an events planner has received a post high school education, usually at a recognized college or university. There are two-year and four-year colleges offering degrees, and graduate programs as well as certificate programs and noncredit courses available. A formal education is not absolutely essential to be successful because people can learn on the job with a high school education, particularly those with years of specialized training experience in an aspect of events planning. But at larger corporations and hotel/resort conglomerates, a degree confers a minimum level of understanding and experience. A corporation or major hotel/resort may only seek an events planner with a college degree.

If this is a second career then one consideration is a certificate program offered by a well-recognized university or college. Often universities that offer baccalaureate and masters degree programs will provide certificate programs for those unwilling or unable to commit to a full-scale degree program.

If someone just wants to understand more about events planning and is uncertain if this is the right career choice, noncredit courses at a university or college's School of Continuing Education are an inexpensive way to learn more. It may also be a way of learning from other students the potential career opportunities available in the local area. It is advisable to check with the School of Continuing Education whether noncredit students are eligible to utilize the services of the college's Career Placement Office.

There are several educational paths to pursue so the dilemma for an aspiring events planner is in which educational direction to head. Those who prefer working in a corporate or trade association environment are probably best served by focusing on events planning as the specialty. However, if one is considering a career working in the non-profit world then there are two distinct avenues for training: events planning or the more generic non-profit management. If the ultimate occupational prize is to obtain a senior position in a non-profit rather than aspiring to a senior position in a corporation including the hotel/resort industry, then a degree in non-profit management is potentially a better educational investment.

One never knows, even after a few years in a particular occupation, if this is the desired profession or more importantly in the events planning business whether to exclusively work in a non-profit versus for-profit environment. The most beneficial aspect of being in the events planning field is the relative ease of moving from one industry to another, and from the for-profit to the non-profit worlds.

Although undergraduate and certificate programs are easily available for the study of non-profit management, the most prestigious degree is certainly the Masters degree. And there are several complementary educational choices on this graduate level.

Two-Year Colleges
Events Planning

The choices of where to obtain an associate degree are vast. If time and money is limited there are established programs at public community colleges across the country. Public community colleges are usually affordable. There are private, non-profit and for profit colleges offering associate degrees. What you need to do is compare the cost of the education with the placement opportunities available at the end of the journey. Ask about where graduating students are finding placements. Also inquire about starting salaries and the availability of internships.

The particular degree offered by a two-year college can vary but typically it's an Associate Degree of Applied Science in Hotel & Restaurant Management. Some of these programs are geared towards restaurant management and include a majority of classes on sanitation and food service courses. If this is not how you want to enter the events planning business then make certain that there are some classes in meeting management and that the college encourages and provides internships, particularly paid internships. Look for a public two-year college that offers expansive career opportunities in: lodging, food service, resort operation, sports facility operation, tourism marketing, special events and festivals.

Four-Year Colleges/Universities
Events Planning

Both public and private four-year colleges offer degrees. Below are examples of universities known for their events planning curriculum. A university such as Johnson & Wales in Rhode Island is a recognized leader in the hospitality industry. Johnson & Wales offers baccalaureate degrees in:

- Baking & Pastry Arts & Food Service Management

- Culinary Arts and Food Service Management
- Hotel & Lodging Management
- International Hotel & Tourism Management
- Restaurant, Food and Beverage Management
- Sports/Entertainment/Event Management
- Travel, Tourism & Hospitality Management.

The Rosen College of Hospitality Management of the University of Central Florida is a public university, which offers a Bachelor of Science in:

- Hospitality Management
- Event Management
- Restaurant & Foodservice Management
- Certificate Program in Event Management

One of the centers of world entertainment and special events is probably Las Vegas, Nevada. As expected, the University of Nevada, Las Vegas's Harrah Hotel College offers a Meeting & Events Management Program, which encompasses the entire spectrum of events planning including conferences, conventions, tradeshows, special events and entertainment. The program studies events planning from A to Z and most of the classes are on-line.

Non-profit Management

More than a hundred public and private universities and colleges offer one or more courses in non-profit management on the undergraduate level. Approximately, forty percent offer three or more courses. The training's focus is preparing students for positions in the human services or youth agency fields and not in events planning. Graduates usually fill entry-level professional positions in non-profit organizations. Many of these undergraduate programs are welcoming to the older returning student or someone in need of re-training because of shifting economic conditions.

In addition, 70 colleges and universities are affiliated with a program called the Non-profit Leadership Alliance (formerly American Humanics), which provides a national certification program. The goal of this organization is to "strengthen the social sector with a talented, prepared workforce." These are both public and private institutions of higher learning in 33 states around the country. It is a collaborative venture that includes academia and the non-profit world. Through non-profit partners such as the American Red Cross, The Arc, Big Brothers Big Sisters, Boy Scouts of America, Boys & Girls Clubs, Camp Fire USA, students receive internships and placement opportunities. There are also scholarships available.

Certificate Programs
Events Planning

Already a college graduate and you are not interested in starting from the beginning in the educational process? A host of well-known universities offer certificate programs. The number of classes required differs from program to program as does where the training takes place. The content of the core courses is similar: Event Management, Event Marketing.

Recognizing that people may be interested in event planning while actively working in another field more and more universities are offering courses on-line. As to be expected, tuition costs vary.

Non-profit Management

If a career in the non-profit sector is the real catalyst for working in events planning but that career choice is still a little fuzzy than a Certificate in Non-profit Management is an appropriate choice. This is particularly true for someone who already holds a baccalaureate degree. It often does not make good financial sense to return to obtain another baccalaureate degree. A large number of colleges and universities offer certificate programs in non-profit management. Many of these programs operate from Schools of Continuing Education/Studies. The difference between a certificate program and a collection of noncredit courses is that the school has organized the courses into a package that in their view constitutes a standard level of knowledge. For example, a university may offer several courses, which taken together constitute a Certificate in Non-profit Management. Typical courses are:

- o   Strategic Management
- o   Financial Management
- o   Marketing Management
- o   Non-profit Governance
- o   Operations Management
- o   Fundraising Management.

In this type of curriculum, an Events Planning course would be just a minor study. Most of the non-profit management programs do not appear to delve into the details necessary to actually learn enough about planning and managing events.

<u>Noncredit Courses</u>
Events Planning

Usually, these courses are offered through a college or university's School of Continuing Education or Professional Studies program and provide a taste of what a career may require. It is the first step for someone who is uncertain that this is their chosen occupational path. For someone without experience in the field, this is a first step before investing heavily in formal higher education.

Non-profit Management

Available courses in non-profit management include titles such as

- Fundraising
- Managing Your Non-profit Organization
- Board of Directors Governance
- Leadership Ethics
- Non-profit Finance

<u>Masters Degrees</u>

An events planner looking to greatly expand their expertise in the non-profit sector and already possess a baccalaureate degree should consider a graduate degree with a concentration in non-profit management. A Masters degree is not a good investment for someone who loves events planning and wants to simply earn more money. That individual might consider becoming a private consultant and starting their own events planning business.

For the individual, who wants to become a director or executive of a non-profit and not work in the for-profit sector, then the Masters degree opens doors. Interestingly, non-profit management has several different avenues of higher education to explore. There are more than 150 different colleges and universities in the US offering Masters degrees with a concentration in non-profit management.

Schools of Business are one place to find non-profit management majors. According to US News and World Report, the best business schools offering a non-profit management concentration are: Yale University, Stanford University, University of California – Berkeley (Haas), Northwestern University (Kellogg), University of Michigan – Ann Arbor (Ross), Duke

University (Fuqua), University of Pennsylvania (Wharton), Columbia University and New York University (Stern).

The purported strengths of a business degree in non-profit management are:

- Established performance record of teaching management including organizational management
- Similarities exist between business entities and non-profits as more non-profits strive to incorporate business principles
- Prestige of a MBA degree – transferability to other industries

Schools of Public Administration are another educational option. The MPA course of study fills in the gaps of the MBA. The question is whether non-profits and businesses are so common, sharing similar values and goals that the different orientation remains a neat fit. The relative strengths of the MPA center on the purported similarities between non-profits and government versus business and non-profits.

- Similar values and jargon
- Public managers and non-profit managers both learn to deliver services to meet community needs
- Careers intertwine – public servants becoming non-profit managers and the reverse

There are more options for the potential non-profit manager. Often Schools of Social Work offer a concentration in non-profit management. While there are common threads between social work and the non-profit sector these institutions of higher learning often lack the managerial expertise of other types of graduate schools. Also there is the subjective image that a MPA

11

or MBA degree is more prestigious than a MSW. In addition, there is the highly specific, independent Masters of Non-profit Organization (MNO). The criticism of these programs is that they are too restrictive and lack occupational elasticity potentially limiting the degree holder from readily switching to public service or business.

The skills necessary to be successful in the field

A successful events planner has developed a coterie of skills that would be enviable in many other occupations. This is a stressful occupation and requires a methodical individual with excellent organizational skills. It is a logistics-oriented, detailed type of work. The successful events planner is a person comfortable and adept at multi-tasking and one with well-honed verbal and written communication skills.

The diversity of activities required to be a successful events planner means that the individual must be an excellent communicator. This is important because the events planner will be writing, editing, correcting copy for all manner of materials whether it's save the date postcards, formal invitations, instructions to vendors, reviewing contracts as well as advertising, Web site announcements, newsletters, thank you notes, and a report to the boss after the event.

Verbal skills are also essential. The event planner must communicate with a large variety of people from vendors, to Senior Management, to staff. Meeting and working closely with strangers is part of the job description and the ability to work closely with these new associates is important for the event to be successful. Since events planning is one filled with hundreds of details to juggle, clarity in both verbal and written communications facilitates the process.

Inarticulate messages confuse and can lead to delays, mistakes and costly overcharges.

Increasingly, quantitative skills are becoming part of the event planner's professional resume. Comfort with using figures and spreadsheets are required, not necessarily at the level of an actuary or mathematician, but understanding financials is part of the job. Do you possess the ability to work with numbers? Financial skills are necessary to construct and manage budgets. Negotiating contracts with vendors whether in selecting the venue or the meal choices means understanding financial details. Is the vendor giving you a financial discount? Can the event turn a profit? Conducting the after-event audit contrasts the expenses against the revenue.

Determining the success of an event requires number crunching. Familiarity and the ability to utilize measurement and evaluation techniques are part of the expanding skill sets of an events planner. This requires learning some market research methods: quantitative survey design and implementation as well as the use of focus groups to measure more qualitative reactions.

The events planner is a marketer and media savvy. Events may never be open to the public but even internal events require the ability to write ad copy or press releases.

Multi-tasking demands an organized mind and hopefully one that maintains organized files whether in a file cabinet or in the computer. Deadlines are so important it's the "planner" in events planning. Project C can't proceed without the completion of Project A. So a logical mind is essential to keep all the juggling balls in place.

What are the career opportunities for event planners?

The federal government's Department of Labor calculates that this is a growing occupation with good income and job potential. During the next decade, the employment potential will grow twenty percent. Despite the increasing use of video conferencing and other glitzy technology, the face-to-face meeting is an important communications medium. In an age of frugality, meetings may become less frequent but they will not disappear.

According to the federal Department of Labor, the increase in new forms of communication will, in fact, lead to a greater demand for in-person meetings. Scattered operational sites and employees who have offices in their own homes require opportunities for associates to meet and discuss ideas, celebrate important organizational milestones and learn new directives. In addition, as technology and new information proliferates, staff needs constant refresher courses. Some can be handled on-line but not all respond well to distance learning. Or as staff becomes better educated, credentialing authorities may require more continuing education credits to maintain certification or licensure.

One of the virtues of being an events planner is that the skills are usually transferable between companies and among the various types of non-profits. That gives events planners an enviable flexibility, and therefore, they are not as susceptible to the usual cyclical ups and downs. For example, someone working as an event planner in the arts field can switch to a social service agency or become a corporate events planner or work for government.

According to the federal government, (US Bureau of Labor Statistics), the median annual earnings of meeting and convention planners in 2014 was $46,490. Experienced planners earned $82,060 while beginners start at $26,000. (These figures are national so can vary from region to region).

Consulting Firms – Become an Entrepreneur

Is it time to move on and start your own business? One of the benefits of being a successful events planner is that it is possible to start one's own consulting firm. The typical route is becoming an expert on at least some aspect of events planning such as catering or hotel/resort management and join forces with someone with complementary skills to form a partnership. This is discussed in the book including the basics for anyone considering starting their own events planning business.

Audience for this Book: Expert, Novice, Considering the Career

Are you an events planner? Or do you aspire to become an events planner? This is the book for you. It is a handy guide for experienced events planners searching for a few better ideas. It's a resource guide for the novice addressing a wide range of topics. It's an excellent manual for the individual exploring the career to understand the occupational responsibilities and expectations. This "Introduction" provides important information on training and skills development as well as employment prospects. But there is much, much more.

Purpose of this Book

The book serves as a comprehensive checklist of what to do, when to do it, how to do it and after the event examining what went right and improvements for the future. The book's chapters examine in detail specific types of events.

- Conferences
- Galas
- Dining – Breakfast, Lunch & Dinner
- Sporting Events: Golf, Tennis, Sailing, Walkathons and other "a-thons"
- Sport Outings
- Theatre Outings
- Groundbreakings & Ribbon Cuttings
- Employee-centered Events

Each chapter contains "Helpful Hints" that may just make the event easier. No two events are completely alike but understanding the common threads and patterns will help so that each new event is not a totally new experience.

While events vary in length, cost, complexity, they also contain kennels of similarities. There are a core of activities and ideas that are central to any event. These fundamental components will be discussed in detail. Each chapter will discuss:

- Goal or Purpose of the Event
- Frequency of the Event – annual, quarterly, monthly
- Timeline - Deadlines
- Audience
- Public Invited
- Press Invited
- Importance of Location
- Importance of the Date
- Establishing Special Committees
- Preferred vendors or competitive bidding
- Menu
- Decorations

- Entertainment
- Awards/Gifts
- Seating Arrangements
- Communications – snail mail, e-mail, text messaging, Twitter, Web-based
- Marketing of Event
- Public Relations

The budget is so all important that a chapter will be dedicated to understanding how to develop an event budget and manage it. One focus will be on the temptations to go over-budget and the consequences of doing so.

Chapter 2 Secrets of Success:
Universal Logistics

Since the purpose of this book is to offer suggestions that can assist in mitigating potential pitfalls, we start with the first secret of success – details matter. Events planning is a compilation of many and varied pieces of information coming together in just the right package to create a successful event. The type of information is multi-faceted. When one is down in the trenches trying to make sense of all the variant items it's difficult to see the end product.

That brings us to the second secret of success – create a detailed written plan. This is not a 'to-do' list. Even small events require detailed planning. One of the big differences between a 'to-do' list and an actual plan, which results in success rather than recrimination, is distinguishing between the most important activities and those of lesser importance. No detail is ever unimportant. Use a computer, use a blackboard, use a notebook but create the steps to be accomplished, track their progress and cross them off when completed.

Successfully juggling the logistics in the plan's design is the third secret. Learn immediately if there is adequate staff for managing and controlling the logistics. Often this translates into not enough human bodies to accomplish all the details in the plan. Is there an adequate number of staff with the right experience?

Secret number four, "Stick to the timeline." This is always likely to be a problem. So what's the alternative? Every responsible plan has to have some wiggle room for meeting timelines and options if activity A fails to be met before Activity B. All time sensitive objectives need a reasonable grace period in some cases it can be a week or sometimes it's only 24 hours. The best plans can maneuver through unexpected delays or price increases. Crazy things can happen: the vendor of choice goes bankrupt, key staff leave, there's a fire.

An annual event can have the "already done that" feel. Success secret number five is to keep all events, even the smallest, possess a quality of uniqueness. You can't please everybody but a vast majority of participants should be able to report that the event was worthwhile attending. It is not easy to construct a creative event every time but a sense of "deja vu" diminishes the appeal and success of an event. Events and organizations have diverse measures of what constitutes different. The overall guideline is to be different without being bizarre or outrageous. Each organization sets its own institutional parameters of what is considered "bland" and what is considered "too over the top."

Another secret is to know your audience. Nothing kills an event and possibly the career of an events planner as much as the event viewed as inappropriate by the influential inner circle in the organization. The finance department may have a completely different view of refreshing than the Executive Committee of the Board of Directors. Age, gender, race, position in the organization can all be factors in determining an audience's taste. An event that includes most of the organization can be a trickier one to manage than a more homogenous group.

Mother's adage that first impressions matter is another secret of success. The first announcement of the event, the first meeting with senior staff, the first conversation with vendors, the look of the venue when the guests arrive, whatever stands between the entrance into the event and the registration table are all potential points where first impressions matter. Remember that first impressions are difficult to rescind.

One of the secrets of success for planning the next event is conducting a thorough evaluation of the last event. The evaluation should include the opinions of as many guests as possible. One way to handle this is to provide through anonymous techniques such as surveys on the table or by the exit doors, on-line Web site, a suggestion box back at headquarters. Don't forget to ask the opinions and comments of your vendors; perhaps there is a way to make the relationship smoother. You also want comments and opinions and suggestions for improvements from your staff. Every event should include as part of the detailed plan a debriefing session within a reasonable period of time after the event. It's difficult to recall the small details that would improve the management of an event or a great idea that should be retained after more than a week. Participants in the debriefing can include a variety of guests, staff, and senior management.

To Recap the Secrets of Success:

- Details matter
- Create a detailed written plan
- Juggling the logistics
- Stick to the timeline
- Be creative
- Know you audience
- First impressions matter
- Thorough evaluation

Chapter 3 Budget: *Spending Wisely*

Here's where the events planner's financial skills are tested – preparing and keeping to the budget. It doesn't require the skills of an accountant but do be prepared to create numerous number crunching versions based on different financial scenarios. And it is essential to be able to track all expenses both large and small. Few events are provided open-ended budgets. In most cases, the events planning staff starts with a budget. If it's a reoccurring event it probably looks similar to last year's budget. If one is fortunate, there's an upwards cost of living adjustment increasing the budget size by a few percentage points. Hopefully, this captures all vendor and other cost increases.

Helpful Hints
Set Realistic Budget
Consensus by budget stakeholders
Make as few modifications as possible
Keep to the Budget
Keep Good Records
Audit the Actual versus the Projected

The greatest danger is the failure to prepare a realistic budget and then being forced to make modifications. The unforeseen is always possible. For example, cost cutting at the organization leads to last minute budgetary cuts after the original budget has been approved. The events planner is then in the precarious situation of having to make unplanned cuts. Hopefully, this does not result in drastic cost cutting but making smaller slices, eliminating the nice and keeping necessary.

In preparing the budget think of contingencies. A budget should provide a cushion should vendors' costs unexpectedly rise; it is prudent to build-in a cushion.

Who does the events planner need to consult for budgetary approval? How involved is this person(s) in preparing the budget? Is it the events planner or someone else in the organization or a shared responsibility? Regardless of who signs off on the budget, the events planner is responsible for ensuring that costs do not exceed the allocated budget.

Who are the budget stakeholders? Are they different individuals than those providing input into the actual developing and running of the event? Is the individual or group responsible for signing the checks involved in reviewing the budget prepared by the events planner? And do they include people outside the organization such as external consultants or Board members who are not actively involved in the organization's normal business activities.

Unless the event is completely different than anything ever attempted in the past, the new budgetary process starts by analyzing last year's budget. Usually, this means basing this year's budget on last year's unless there are compelling reasons such as cost cutting or budgetary expansion. The more detailed the budget the easier it is to conduct a thorough analysis. By reviewing last year's expenses it is possible to gauge the accuracy of the budget process. Technology costs should be getting smaller and liquor costs larger.

There are typical standard categories of expenses based on:

- Purpose of the event (i.e., educational conference, gala, sports outing, all staff training)
- Number of attendees
- Length of time (i.e., two-hours versus two weeks)
- Choice of venue (i.e., company offices versus Disneyland)
- Time of the year (i.e., peak periods such as holiday party or summertime outdoor event or non-peak)

Depending upon the size and type of event, expense tracking can be accomplished by using common computer software such as Excel or purchase any of the specifically designed events planning software available. Some software companies permit a potential purchaser to test it out. If a big event is coming soon and there's software worth testing then seek permission for a free 30-day trial.

One of the first budgetary items under consideration is whether the events planning staff will completely run the event or will be supplemented by consultants. A small staff or an inexperienced staff can lead to the sensible decision to use an events planning consulting firm.

Meeting planners working for hotels/resorts who have non-profit clients will often be working with volunteers from the non-profit. These volunteers can be helpful or they can be problematic but they must be included in the planning. They can sometimes be very effective substitutes for paid staff and represent an important budgetary saving.

Some very particular types of events can be run more effectively than others with outside support. For example, there are several firms just devoted to running golf tournaments. A golf event is a logistical headache. There's the right venue, 18 holes, celebrities, contests; it can be simpler to let a highly specialized firm handle it.

Variable & Fixed Costs

Accounting practices separate fixed from variable costs. It helps for planning the event to use this distinction especially if the total number of attendees is subject to change from year to year or event to event.

The fixed costs are immutable – they don't change if the event is meant for 50 or 500. A typical fixed cost is the rental for the venue site although with proper planning and past experience one wouldn't rent a site that holds 500 when the expected attendance is 50. However, mistakes like these are made when the potential audience is highly unpredictable (e.g., first-time event, completely new staff, unrealistic expectations by events planner or more senior executives). Other common fixed expenses are items such as security, insurance, and the entertainment. If you hire the singer or the band they get paid whether anyone shows up for the event or the place is packed.

The variable costs fluctuate based on attendance size. The dining costs are based on per person fees. The number of invitations printed, postage, tables, decorations, tents is variable. It may be possible to reduce per person unit costs as the number of attendees rises. There can be "price points."

Certain expenses can be either variable or fixed based on the vendor. For example, transportation expenses such as parking can be a fixed cost at one venue or per vehicle at a different venue. With some number crunching one can determine which is financially better and consider this as a factor in selecting a venue.

Projected or Budgeted Expense versus Actual Cost

Costs can change in mid-stream. They can rise or fall depending upon circumstances, usually unintended. Often this can happen as attendance reaches a certain threshold and per unit costs can decline. The result can also happen that an audience is smaller than expected and costs per person rise. Vendors usually have a clause in their contracts about a 10% differential meaning the contract must be honored if costs rise by 10 percent.

An appropriate analysis of the event will always include projected/budgeted expense versus actual. The variance between projected and actual expenses should not be more than 10 percent. That is why good budget preparation should result in expenses coming in close to the projected amount. And it is never healthy if the total projected budget is significantly different than the actual budget. Something has gone amiss if that happens.

Budget Categories

Part of developing a sound budget is being able to capture all expenses. Past experience is a handy guide but not always reassuring in unpredictable times.

The standard categories are listed below. Every event will not include every item but analyzing every possible expense is better than mistakenly missing a category and leaving an expense unaccounted for in the budgetary process.

Venue

Most event budgets start with the venue. Often this is the most expensive single item. The choice of a venue is often decided by the purpose or goal of the event. Is it a small, cozy event for 50 or a five-course dinner for 500? It can also be influenced by a senior member of the company.

Research and select appropriate Venue

Unless this is a first time event, start the selection process by reviewing last year's venue. Was it a satisfactory experience or were there problems? Were these serious problems or the usual run of complaints from attendees augmented by sterling compliments?

If you are the events planner for the hotel/resort that hosted the event, I would want to know how clients viewed the experience. I would want to know the experiences of every event client – small or large. It is important to get feedback.

Some venues are capable of hosting a great event whether it's large or small. For a company events planner if there are several events of varying sizes during the year, a venue with multiple offerings can be a convenient choice. The venue staff gets to know the events planning staff and a rapport is developed, which can make the events run smoother.

If I am the hotel/resort events planner, I want to be able to create the best possible events package for any client that requires multiple events. There's always competition so how does my hotel/resort stand out from others? One certain winning appeal is a great financial package that respects client loyalty.

How do venues differ? Fashionable hotels in the middle of large cities can offer a fabulous setting but if transportation access is a problem then it's one issue to consider. If most people will be arriving by car then easy access to major highways is a consideration. And if the venue is in the heart of a city is accessible, safe and convenient public transportation available?

Consider at least three venues for each major event. Beyond re-evaluating last year's venue, research can begin with the Internet. Some venues permit a virtual tour of the facility. This is not a substitute for an actual inspection but it can be a valuable researching technique. Even exclusive hotels/resorts should offer virtual tours.

The first decision about the venue has to do with the right size. You should not cram people into a tight space nor at the other extreme do you want to have an empty feeling by selecting a venue that is too large. Beyond sheer space there may be other spatial requirements (e.g., high ceilings, soundproof room, shape of the room – square versus rectangular or circular). Evaluate all provided amenities and consider those that are nice versus those that are necessary:

- Presence of on-site business center
- Shipping and receiving services
- House phones in meeting rooms
- Availability of concierge services and information desks with qualified, knowledgeable people

Hotel as Venue

Hotels and resorts are the most common venue because they can offer so many amenities and flexibility in designing the event. A hotel with a solid reputation can provide a ballroom, conference rooms, meeting rooms, accommodations and a kitchen menu for every meal. Since they offer so much and so much convenience a hotel/resort can represent the best possible value.

The most serious negative is that few hotels do everything well. A great looking ballroom can be off-set by rather ordinary hotel rooms. In general, hotels are not universally recognized for operating the most innovative kitchens so meals are not usually the selling point. .But if one is looking for the widest range of possible choices then a hotel or resort has a lot to offer. And this fact alone can simplify an event and minimize stress for the corporate events planning staff.

Understanding the many positive features of the hotel or resort compared to other potential venues gives the hotel/resort's events planning staff a genuine advantage. It is the role of each hotel/resort's events planning staff to emphasize the flexibility and many options available, and minimize any shortcomings. Therefore, it is important that the hotel/resort's events planning staff have a realistic understanding of the strengths and weaknesses of their hotel/resort. It is also essential that the hotel/resort events planning staff know as much as possible about nearby competitors including other hotels/resorts in a thirty mile radius.

Perform an inspection

No one books a venue without an inspection. And it's a good idea to unexpectedly appear without an appointment to just observe when the venue staff is not conducting a tour.

The inspection should involve:

- Conditions of the grounds and landscaping
- Conditions of the carpeting and paint
- Appearance of the public restrooms
- Appropriateness of the décor for the event
- Parking facilities if available
- Adequate room size for the main event and other aspects (i.e., meeting rooms)

- Noise levels inside the event rooms and from the outside
- Flexibility to adjust room layout/tables/dance floor
- Up to date Technology (i.e., audio-visual, sound system)
- Appearance of the hotel rooms for events planning staff, attendees, guests, VIPs
- Extras such as gym, swimming pool, golf course, day care center
- Cleanliness
- Tasty menu choices
- Availability of emergency medical services

Negotiate for best venue rates

No venue is perfect but if the venue can provide most of what a corporate events planner needs for a particular event then negotiating the best venue rates is the challenge. Leveraging is a key component. If many of the year's events can be hosted at this one venue then a good rate is expected and should be demanded.

Leveraging can also provide good value if the corporate events planner is booking the event and needs hotel rooms. A flexible hotel/resort staff will want to sweeten the deal with free meeting rooms or at least reductions in the room rates for attendees and other guests including speakers. The organization may have an existing contract with a particular hotel/resort but still negotiate for a better deal.

Compare line item expense deals offered with package deals. Consider what the package deal encompasses. The package price maybe a better deal because the hotel/resort staff will know exactly where their profit margins are and therefore be willing to offer more attractive pricing.

29

Date of the Event

If there is potential flexibility regarding the date most venues have a non-peak period where pricing is lower. If the season is not negotiable (i.e., must be held during the summer) is the day of the week flexible? Is there a history of holding the event during the work-week versus the week-end?

Book venue

It's important once reasonable negotiating has been concluded to be decisive and book the venue. The contract is now binding for both sides.

Food Services
Menu

Know your audience. Is the food being served a very important feature of the event? If so then this is not where the corporate events planner wants to cut corners. Is this an audience of picky eaters? If so then it's important that the venue offer a full service on-site kitchen operation so that food adjustments can be done immediately. For many, food must be only reasonably tasty and plentiful, with some variety and nothing too exotic or spicy.

Beverages

A potential source of saving is understanding event usage of alcoholic vs. non-alcoholic selections, premium versus house brands. Are attendees expecting premium brands or will house brands be acceptable? Knowing the event audience simplifies the decision-making.

Permit(s)/Licenses

Outdoor events may require street, food and liquor permits. If this is a totally new and different event then the town or city officials will need adequate lead time to assemble and process the paperwork. A key element is providing sufficient liability insurance to meet the requirements of the permit.

Tables/Chairs/Linens/China/Tents/Glasses Plus Utensils Rentals

One of the chief reasons for selecting a hotel/resort for an event is it is unnecessary to rent those tables, chairs, linens, etc. Hotels and resorts can take responsibility for outdoor events on their premises so tents and chairs are not a burden for the corporate event staff. However, sometimes a location is so perfect that the additional work is worth all the trouble. If the event must be very special then a special spot is a requisite.

Rental firms come in all varieties and while most can supply all the tableware as well as the tables and chairs they don't all rent tents or dance floors. If the event is held at a prime time of the year, supplies maybe limited so rent early.

Labor/Gratuities

Itemized invoices should separate out labor costs from other items. Different venues charge different rates. Don't let labor expenses be lost in the quote. Package deals often include them in the pricing but what you want to avoid is surprises if additional charges appear.

Audio-Visual

This category includes microphones for speakers, sound systems for presentations large and small, computer interface equipment, projectors and screens, people and machinery. Some events require the best and others can be fine with twentieth century technology. If state-of-the-art equipment is required then that becomes an important consideration in selecting the venue. If the company has its own audio-visual staff then the events staff should work with them. This staff may be necessary to have on-site for the event. At a minimum, they should serve as the events staff's AV consultants.

Television Monitors

If the actual proceedings are so far away from those sitting in the rear of the room then it may be necessary to set-up TV monitors in key positions in the room. For certain events TV monitors are needed if it's an overflow situation.

Video Players/Recorders/Cameras

Is the event being taped? Will there be a need for a photographer as well as a videographer? Does the company employ people capable of providing these tasks? Again, employees or existing consultants can provide these services. Hotels and resorts can provide a list of referrals. The hotel/resort events planning staff must be certain that any vendors they recommend are reliable and the fees charged reasonable.

Lecterns/podiums

Speakers will probably want to practice or at least see the podium and test the equipment. Podiums come in all varieties. Some are good enough for a Broadway musical and others resemble classroom lecterns. Don't pay for what you don't need.

Conference Requirements for AV

Conferences may have a multitude of AV needs ranging from high end technology to the lowest end. Major addresses can occur in a ballroom followed by smaller break-out rooms for individual presentations. The requirements can be the best computer interface equipment but also the simple: Flip Charts, Blackboards, Electronic Pointers and Marking Pens. Events planners must consult with speakers to adjust requirements to fit their presentations.

Entertainment

If the event is an annual one and if the venue is always similar the memorable can be delivered through the entertainment. But know the audience. How many events have you attended when the greatest negatives were assailed at the entertainment: too coarse, too dull, political, age inappropriate? It can also be one of the most expensive budget categories or one of the least expensive so be prepared to be able to defend your decisions.

Music

Even conferences may require music accompaniment. Again, music should be both event appropriate and audience appropriate. A group loving hip hop may not appreciate a chamber music quartet. However, don't make assumptions. Look at past events for the best clues. If an event has never introduced music the challenge is in deciding what people will enjoy the most without alienating anyone. Music comes in so many different varieties and pricing that this should be a group decision.

Celebrity

Is the presence of a celebrity crucial to the event's success? History and tradition provide the strongest evidence. How big a celebrity? A celebrity can demand one million dollars or more so how is this going to fit into the budget? Celebrities can also be difficult to book unless they have an association with the company.

Stage

If the event includes a musical show, an orchestra or some other kind of presentation requiring a large space then find the right venue. Stages come in all varieties and technical sophistication. Consider the entertainment component when selecting the venue.

Speaker's Fees

Conferences and other events require speakers. Except for government employees, most speakers expect to be paid and can be as expensive as top entertainers. Academics can be less expensive. In the case of federal employees, if they speak representing the federal government then they are barred from receiving speaker's fees but their expenses will need to be paid. Event staff or someone in high standing within the company should have listened to the speaker at a presentation before they are invited to the event. Audio tapes are a substitute but not always as reliable as hearing the speaker first hand.

Activities
Family Activities

These would include activities in which family members participate while the attendee is otherwise engaged. This can include trips to area attractions, shopping at nearby outlet stores, organized educational visits to museums with a docent. The events planner should budget for direct expenses related to the family activities such as admission fees as well as extras that may be required such as shuttle buses and hotel prepared box lunches.

Supplemental Activities for Attendees

If the event has unscheduled play time will other activities need to be scheduled? These activities can be the financial responsibility of the attendees. Examples of these activities are sports such as golf, tennis, biking or field trips, with or without the rest of the family.

Promotion/Advertising

Even events where the public is barred, promotional expenses exist. Costs may be incurred for seeking company IT staff to make announcements on the intranet. A press release is often created for internal events whether or not it is actually forwarded to the outside press.

Banners

Does the event call for special banners? If the longevity of the banner is only meant for the event then incurring high costs may seem like poor financial stewardship. However, companies take pride in their image so it's a balancing act to provide an item that is physically appealing without breaking the bank.

Promotional Items

The souvenirs that are distributed to event attendees are often keepsakes for both those attendees and events staff. Typical items are tee shirts, mugs, pens or other small items. But depending upon the event, these items can include golf clubs, engraved crystal from Ireland, gold-edged plaques.

A common promotional item that becomes an important souvenir is a DVD of the event. Production costs can vary. The events staff can always use these DVDs as chronicles of the history of the event and useful guides for future events.

Public's Presence Incurs Extra Expenses

If a goal of the event is to increase the event's audience among the general public then, naturally, there will be advertising and marketing costs. Advertising is highly costly so be careful with using precious dollars for ads in newspapers, magazines, TV or radio, on the Internet/company's web site. Consider the local cable channel or bus/train posters. Public transportation systems are eager for new funds and rent space at stations, bus stops and on the vehicles themselves.

Instead of expensive advertising, the company should consider free publicity through the writing and forwarding of press releases. However, if the staff is too stretched an additional cost may be incurred by hiring a public relations firm.

Web site

The most cost effective media may be the company's Web site. Again, costs may be incurred by the company's IT staff in creating activity on the Web site. At a minimum, each of the company's events should be posted on the Web site with contact information.

Security

Most venues provide standard security. However, if there's a celebrity present or any political protesting anticipated then it may be prudent to employ a private security firm.

Insurance

Most venues provide their own liability insurance. However, if it's an outdoor event there may be a need for additional insurance. Confer with the company's financial staff or insurance broker for advice.

Graphic Design/Printing

We live in the digital age but practically all events still require printing and potentially graphic design work. The best guide is a similar previous event.

Designer

A large company even with its own graphic design staff may have costs encumbered. Keep track of these expenses. At some point, outside bids for graphic design work can be more cost effective.

Examples of design projects include creation of:

- Brochures
- Media Kit
- Registration Packets
- Posters
- Flyers
- Invitations
- Tickets
- Specialty Items

Keep itemized records for all costs and track these expenses. This is especially important in evaluating last year's event compared to this year's event.

Duplicating

People still like to see and read paper. Expect costs for duplicating items.

Other Types of Printing

The items that follow don't require the special talents of a design team but the expenses should be tracked for present and future reference.

Event/Conference Program
- Corporate Signs
- Event Signage
- Name Tags/Holders
- Place Cards
- Awards/Recognitions/Certificates which also may require engraving costs
- Thank you Cards

Postage/Shipping

E-mail has become the norm but regular snail mail hasn't entirely disappeared. Consider the following expenses

- Postage
- Bulk Mail Permits
- Mail House
- Freight
- Delivery Services

Travel

Travel expenses come in several varieties:

- Attendee travel expenses
- Speaker's travel expenses
- VIP travel
- Mileage Reimbursement by Staff & consultants

To promote a "green event" encourage transportation other than air travel or single occupant auto travel:

- Train

- Staff car pooling
- Limousine
- Car Rental of hybrids

Additional travel expenses to track include:

- Valet Parking
- Shuttles/Buses
- Event transfers

Decorations

What memorable event doesn't come with decorations? These can be large event budget expenses. They can be broken down into major categories:

- Room Decorations (i.e., ballroom, meeting rooms)
- Stage Decorations
- Special Hotel room decorations for VIPs

In addition, decorations can be everywhere else during an event. The common ones to track are:

- Centerpieces for Tables – type of centerpiece
- Flowers/Plants
- Candles
- Balloons
- Signs
- Props

Chapter 4 Conferences

Educational

Collaborations among Business, Academic Institutions, Government & Non-Profits

An educational conference has a host and sponsor(s). Sometimes they are the same organization. However, increasingly non-profits and academic institutions turn to business to provide the bulk of conference funding. In recent years, academic institutions have relied heavily on business or industry groups to sponsor an educational conference while the academic institution arranges for the presentation of the scientific research.

The company or industry group gains prestige through association with the academic institution or academic specialty while these educational non-profits gain financial support. In the absence of government funding, outside business financial support has become the norm. Business and academia have forged valuable symbiotic relationships.

The trick for the events planner is separating the responsibilities of each organization but maintaining cooperation, and the sharing of information and coordinating logistics. Over time, a company can be linked to the sponsorship of a particular educational conference(s) in a similar way that business has relationships with college sports teams (i.e., baseball, football, basketball) or sporting events such as world-class tennis or golf.

Helpful Hints
• To encourage attendance wherever possible provide for Continuing Education Credits for professional licensure/certification
• Federal government employees in their official capacity appear for free although travel expenses may need to be paid
• Controversial subjects can be addressed by providing differing opinions

Educational conferences do vary in length ranging from a breakfast meeting where the latest clinical advice is presented to several days with multiple sessions and presenters. An educational conference where world-wide scientific research data is presented is most likely to be at least three days and potentially more than a week.

Company sponsorships can also vary. The entire one-week educational conference can be sponsored by one company or an industry association, which may be incorporated as a non-profit. Similar to other types of sponsorships, educational conferences can involve one or two major sponsors with a half-dozen minor sponsors. And all expect some visible recognition for their sponsorship dollars.

Educational conferences are platforms for sharing information by a variety of groups:

- Academic specialty associations (i.e., Academy of Political Science, American Agricultural Economics Association)

41

- Medical Specialties (i.e., American Academy of Child and Adolescent Psychiatry, American Academy of Orthopaedic Surgeons)
- Higher education associations (i.e., American Association of Community Colleges, American Association of State Colleges and Universities)
- State-wide Business Associations or State-wide Business & Industry Associations
- National Industry or Trade or Union Associations

In addition, the government will host and sponsor educational conferences for a variety of purposes. Frequent sponsors are federal research organizations such as the National Institutes of Health (NIH) and its many sub-agencies (National Institutes of Environmental Health Sciences, National Cancer Institute). This is their opportunity to create forums and platforms for research funded by the government to be released in a peer-review atmosphere.

In fact, federal organizations issue "Requests for Proposals (RFPs)" to outsource educational conferences to non-profit agencies as well as businesses. A potential revenue source for a non-profit experienced in presenting educational conferences is submitting a grant application in response to a government-issued RFP. The competition is from both for-profit businesses as well as non-profits. An organization with expertise in running educational conferences should check out these opportunities by reviewing the federal grant web site: www.grants.gov. or investigate becoming a federal vendor through the Web site (FedBizOpps-FBO – fbo.support@gsa.gov).

Collaboration

Well run educational conferences are often collaborations between non-profits, academia, business and government. The involvement of business in the educational conferences is a financial one. The academic institution or non-profit hosting the education conference will turn to the business community for outright funding support or discounts on hotels or airlines as well as printing and postage, Internet savvy. The business may also be able to provide logistical know-how on organizing and running the event.

There is a "what's in it for me" mentality when business or a trade association sponsor educational conferences. The business wants to be linked with the research because it confers status, prestige, a marketing advantage.

The sponsorship should come with "no strings attached." Business sponsorships have come under attack in recent years when those business interests interfere with academic freedom and any trace of censorship by the business or trade group.

Businesses which operate research facilities are natural sponsors of educational conferences such as pharmaceutical companies, defense contractors. Again, the potential pitfall is in appearing to influence the scientific results presented by researchers. It lends an air of unacceptable impropriety. That's where the non-profit can assist by its involvement with an educational conference serving as a cushion separating the business interests from the research presentations.

Registration Fees

Even with the financial assistance of a business sponsor registration fees are the norm at educational conferences. A formal agreement between the sponsor and the host conference organization is necessary to delineate roles and responsibilities as well as the disbursement of registration fees. Educational conferences do not have to make a profit but it should not be a financial drain. A government sponsored event may disallow any registration fees.

Professional Credits for Attendance

Many professions require members to receive continuing education credits. Often these professional requirements can be met through attendance at educational conferences. The agency certifying the credits may set demands for the event. Early agreement with the certifying agency is crucial to eliminate attendees experiencing problems with receiving their continuing education credits. The logistics of obtaining continuing education credits is usually the responsibility of the host and not the sponsor. Any conference which offers continuing education credits should advertise and market that fact.

Exhibitors

One method to cover the increasing costs of hosting and sponsoring educational conferences is to share the financial burden with exhibitors. Association and trade groups frequently depend upon exhibitors to defray costs. For the events planning staff this is an additional and burdensome factor but often necessary. At academic educational conferences, sellers of such items as textbooks, computer software and hardware, telecommunications equipment and even athletic equipment are willing exhibitors. Non-profit groups hosting an educational conference can also benefit from soliciting exhibitors. The presence of such exhibitors can provide financial security. Specific exhibitors need to be vetted to ensure that the products and services are reputable. An educational conference does not want to be tarnished because of controversy resulting from the presence of a certain vendor.

Annual Event

Educational conferences can be regional, state-wide, national, and international, and occur annually or biannually. It may be the same time of year every year reflecting academic scheduling or off-season rates. Past conferences are good guides to timing and scheduling.

Specific Theme

Even educational conferences can have themes to differentiate one year from the other. As with any routine event, the theme can reflect milestones – 100th anniversary of the organization, the birthday or anniversary or death of an important figure in the field, great new discovery or commemorating a great old discovery.

Importance of Location

Choosing the venue for an educational conference is one of the more important decisions made by the events planning staff. The real estate adage location, location, location is just as essential to events planning. When working with a national association or organization an important detail is where to hold the event. Locations can be traditional: even numbers on the west coast and odd number years on the east coast. Understandably, a national or international conference will require ready access to airports and major transportation hubs so this needs to be taken into account about the venue choice.

Considerations:

- Politics precludes holding an educational conference at a particular city or in a particular state
- The home state or academic institution of the conference chair hosts the event in their facility

- Government sponsorship results in the conference held at or near appropriate government facility
- Conference location has no restrictions
- Conference must be held in the USA

Importance of Date/Time of Year

The timing of the educational conference can be set by school calendar, always standard vacation times or never vacation periods. How much flexibility is permitted impacts the budget. It's less expensive to hold the educational conference in the Caribbean in August than January or go to Minneapolis in December than August.

Closed or Open to the Public

Most educational conferences are open to the public although not likely to attract a general interest audience. The events planning staff should contact the public relations or government affairs offices of either the academic host or the company sponsor to check on rules dealing with the presence of the press.

If the public is encouraged to attend is the educational conference advertised? Advertising is expensive but press releases is a less expensive alternative. If the conference will be announcing new research findings, all major media need to be invited since most newspapers, magazines, TV and radio stations, Internet outlets now have some type of "science desk."

Friends/Family Invited

Even academic types bring along their family and friends to educational conferences especially if the location is conductive to family-type activities. This can be a small or rather expansive burden for the events planning staff.

Basic questions that need addressed
:

- Family members invited or encouraged to attend?
- Family members permitted to attend every function and activity?
- Are children allowed to attend?
- What kind of family-oriented activities need to be offered?
- Are family activities always separate from conference attendees' activities?

Entertainment Aspects

Entertainment can be expensive but adds that extra nice touch to the proceedings. Suggestions for less expensive entertainment:

- Local college music department – orchestra, band, chorus
- Major music colleges (i.e., Julliard, Eastman, Curtis, Peabody, Manhattan School of Music, San Francisco Conservatory of Music, University of Indiana) provide a large variety of entertainment through the school's booking agency that includes current students, former students, faculty
- Community orchestras and chorales
- High school marching band, jazz band, school orchestra, chorus
- Local community groups such as dance studio, cheerleading squad

Speakers

The highlight of the educational conference can be an award dinner with guest speaker(s). It can be a world renowned scholar, who may not be a scintillating public speaker; a motivational speaker; politician with a keen interest in the scientific field; or the speaker is one of the growing number of billionaires supporting science through their own private foundations.

Sales Conference

Most major companies hold annual sales conferences to reward and honor those who have significantly made financial contributions to the company. And usually these are lash affairs culminating with an expensive gala where spouses are invited to attend. The ranks of the entire senior staff are invited and attend. Sometimes the Board of Directors is invited.

Often these conferences are used as opportunities to announce new products or services. These can be lavish events with high priced entertainment. The press may be invited for the new product development announcements probably not the dinner.

Most of the detailed information discussed above for educational conferences is applicable. The following needs to be considered for a Sales Conference:

- Specific Theme
- Importance of location
- Importance of Date & Time of the Year
- Closed or Open to the Public
- Friends/Family Invited
- Entertainment
- Speakers

The conference usually ends with a lavish gala. The Gala as an event will be discussed as a separate chapter.

Chapter 5 GALA

For many organizations the event of the year is the Gala. For a sales and marketing-oriented company, it is the most prestigious event and few expenses are spared. It is a reward to those who have earned the highest sales commissions, brought in the most new clients, for new sales staff who have accomplished great sales returns. For the company events planning staff it is how they will be judged.

Most non-profits depend upon the largesse of business to support their annual galas. Sometimes this requires the involvement of company events planning staff and coordination with the non-profit events planning staff.

The event of the year

Helpful Hints
• For the company what's in it for us to support the non-profit & become sponsors
• Originality is hard to maintain but vital for success
• People are eager to attend but still make it pleasantly memorable
• Timelines matter
• Does everyone know their responsibilities six months before the event, 30 days before, the day before and the night of the gala

	• Menus rarely matter just don't poison anyone
	• Flowers and table decorations rarely matter
	• Linens never matter unless they are cost-free
	• May require a Gala Committee that represents Sales & Marketing Executives

The career of an events planner is often determined by the success of the gala. Organizations reminiscent about the great ones and may laugh or cry about the disastrous ones where everything went wrong. Murphy's Law lives in gala planning and implementation – anything that can go wrong, will.

Every events planner wants to be responsible for a great gala. Expectations vary with the person but a rule of thumb is that every great gala should in some way exceed expectations. Look back in the organization's history to discover the secrets of the great galas. Ask long-time staff to indicate which galas were considered successful and which were deemed failures. For example, are there pictures from previous galas lining the walls of the company's headquarters and does one particular gala receive more attention?

Fundraising—working with Non-Profits & Community Groups

A gala, which is the major fundraising event of the season, is obviously going to be measured by financial success although there are other measures of success. In general, success includes:

- Total amount of money raised

- Actual revenue (minus expenses and excluding in-kind donations)
- Number of those attending
- Number of new faces attending
- Increased publicity through free notices in major media

The business community may be involved in the success of a non-profit organization's gala through its sponsorship of the event. All major companies and many small businesses are asked to be sponsors. Company events planning staff may be involved in certain aspects of running the gala. Most hotels/resorts events planning staff will be at some point involved in hosting and assisting a non-profit's gala.

The importance of the gala to a non-profit or community group can often be attributed to its place in the organization's history. Some organizations never hold galas. Organizations that hold galas typically do so on an annual basis although it should not be a given that a gala is held each year. The prime reason the gala is an annual event is because for many organizations it is the most important fundraiser of the year.

Gift Scale

The gift scale is a simple way non-profits and community groups determine how much money is expected to be raised by the gala. It is nothing more than a chart detailing fundraising levels and how many donors will give by those various amounts. The different levels or tiers can be adjusted although there should not be too many. The dollar differences between each level or tier should be logical and easy to follow.

The majority of the money raised for a gala is not from selling individual tickets but generous sponsors buying tables and providing other gifts. Usually, the higher dollar value of each level or tier translates into fewer numbers of sponsors.

See the example below.

GIFT SCALE

	Gifts Needed	Value	Total	Cumulative
Platinum	*4*	*$10,000*	*$40,000*	*$40,000*
Gold	*5*	*$7,500*	*$37,500*	*$77,500*
Silver	*6*	*$5,000*	*$30,000*	*$107,500*
Bronze	*10*	*$2,500*	*$25,000*	*$132,500*
Friends	*20*	*$1,000*	*$20,000*	*$152,500*
Individual Sales	*100*	*$150*	*$15,000*	*$167,500*

Tiers or levels are usually named and the labels can be more imaginative than platinum, gold, silver and bronze. It just has to be understandable to sponsors. A sea-oriented scale such as Fleet Admiral, Admiral, Captain, Commander, Lieutenant and Ensign is interesting for the right type of organization or theme of the gala.

Companies, small and large, will at some point be asked to be a sponsor of a non-profit or community group's gala. For each tier there should be a certain level of benefits. Clearly, the more money requested should be accompanied with more benefits. For example, highest tier gets the most tickets, best seating if there's entertainment. If there's an auction, early viewing of auction items. And most important of all, the most publicity .A top tier sponsor should expect that their name will be on all public relation materials, on the Web site, in all flyers, programs, banners, everywhere.

Cash Flow

Business sponsors should understand that gala vendors want to be paid as much as half the expenses in advance, which is sometimes sooner than the cash flow from donations. Don't be surprised if the non-profit or community group ask for that sponsorship fee or donation well in advance of the event.

Theme

Exciting should be the word to describe the gala – positive adjectives. Each year requires new and fresh thinking. Creativity demands that a few minds get together and brainstorm. Bizarre and weird may be acceptable among certain groups but "new" should not necessarily mean too different. Dinner and dancing gets old especially if the same people attend yearly. So a great gala, hoping to attract a wide and diverse community, has to be able to distinguish itself from all the other galas.

Start the process by reviewing information about other non-profit or community group galas that have occurred in the last 12 months. This is easy to obtain from reading the society pages of newspapers and magazines as well as perusing Web sites of corporate and non-profit organizations. Additionally, go on-line and see what the latest fashion styles and trends are for the year. Use fashion magazines to see the latest colors. Even paint companies such as Sherwin Williams or Dutch Boy also highlight the colors of the year.

One of the easiest themes to develop is around dates that have historical significance. These can include the organization's 25th anniversary, 50th anniversary, and 100th anniversary. It can be the 100th birthday of the organization's founder, 10th anniversary of the death of the founder. Some years have general historical value in terms of the country so use these as potential themes such as the Gettysburg Address by President Lincoln, end of major wars, enactment of major legislation (i.e., enactment of 1964 Civil Rights Act or 1974 creation of the Environmental Protection Agency). Consider scientific discoveries as points of interest in creating the theme. Equally important are themes that are taboo for some reason. Check organizational history to preclude anything that raises hackles.

Timeline

Nothing can be more important in managing an event such as a gala than a realistic timeline and following it. Somewhere in the office, posted in a very visible place, should be that timeline. Every day the events planning staff should be studying it. Timing glitches can be costly – waiting too long to secure the location, problems with invitations. Time is always a consideration. One of the great advantages of today's world is the Internet and its fast-paced delivery. Use it as much as possible.

Becoming a Sponsor

Community groups and non-profit organization need sponsors to ensure a financially successful gala. The sponsors buy the tables, buy auction items, and buy ads in journal books. Big sponsors are honored at the event. Why should your business sponsor an event? Every company events planner should ask themselves what's in it for my company? How does this event enhance and positively promote my company in the hearts and minds of company staff, the Board of Directors, and company clients?

Learn about past sponsors to determine if it's a good fit. Was a competitor the chief sponsor last year? Can the organization show you results from the previous year? How many people attended? Any descriptions of those attending (i.e., age gender, income, where they live).

As a Sponsor Joining Organization's Gala Committee

Events planning staff of the company sponsor(s) may be asked to join the community group or non-profit's Gala Committee. It can be time consuming so consider the benefits both to your employer, the company sponsor, and yourself. What potential knowledge can be gained by my involvement?

The perfect committee is one where half the members are either wealthy enough to buy most of the tables or have friends in that category. The other half of that perfect committee is represented by competent worker bees. They are not afraid to handle the most unpleasant tasks soliciting the money/gifts/donations, finding the sponsors, selling the tables/journal ads, calling vendors, friends and influential members of the community. They work on decorations, seating arrangements, gift bags, sit at the registration desk and take charge of the silent auction.

You must ask yourself are there activities that I would like to learn about? Is my personal participation on the Gala Committee going to open up new contacts for me? Can my employer benefit from my involvement either at this gala or for some future event? Is participating on a non-profit or community group Gala Committee going to teach me something I can use for a future company gala?

Honorees

As a major sponsor of a community group or non-profit's gala a specific company employee (i.e., company president, volunteer of the year) can be an honoree or the company itself is the honoree. If this is part of the gala planning then the company should have a representative on the Gala Committee. Here is where some involvement from the sponsoring company's events planning staff is expected. The company events planning staff should be involve in menu choices, seating arrangements, and possible gifts for the honoree.

At a company gala honorees can be members of the company staff/sales associates or members of the community. Often a company will use a gala as a formal means of recognizing the worthy activities of a community group or non-profit as well as just noteworthy people (i.e., Scholarship winner, Firefighter of the Year, Teacher of the Year, etc.).

Master- Mistress of Ceremonies -- MC

A gala does not need a paid MC or a celebrity. The MC's role should be determined by the theme or historical precedent. Someone associated with the organization can serve in the role of a MC.

The use of a MC celebrity rests in the hope that this individual will be an appealing attraction, make the event more memorable. The person does not have to be connected to the organization but that adds to the uniqueness if there is a specific connection. It can simply be the person who serves as the company's public spokesperson in its marketing or advertising campaign.

Closed or Open to the Public

Any gala can be a closed event for a variety of reasons including the privacy of those attending. Typically, galas that are not fundraising events are open only to a targeted audience. Despite the fact that the public is not invited the company may decide to invite the press. These are decisions not made by events planning staff.

Audience

Is this an invited guest list where attendance is mandatory? In that case, it is important to create a memorable event so that people who feel compelled to attend, nonetheless, enjoy the gala. Knowing exactly who attends can make it easier to choose a venue, plan the menu, determine seating and entertainment.

Entertainment Aspects

There is an expectation of entertainment at a gala whether it's for dancing after dinner or a concert. Entertainment costs can vary dramatically. Knowing the tastes of the audience should influence entertainment decisions. Young people may find 1940's swing music interesting but not entertaining. An older group may find the lyrics to rap music insulting. The extremes are easy to detect it's the subtleties that matter. For a gala celebrating a company milestone it may be appropriate to hire a name brand entertainer and spend one million dollars.

Certain types of performers can be both reasonable and highly entertaining. For example, university level music schools (e.g., Juilliard, Hartt School of Music at the University of Hartford, Berklee School of Music and New England Conservatory in Boston, etc.) often have several options available to events planning staff – student performers (classical, contemporary, jazz, and opera) and graduates who can be hired through the booking services of the music school. Small scale entertainment is available from an amazing variety of sources in the community (e.g., local choral groups and chorales, children's choruses, musical-style singing groups, community orchestras). Enjoyable entertainment does not have to be expensive.

The Internet is a terrific place to start to look for talent. Many entertainers today use the Internet as their publicity arm preferring to directly schedule dates and eliminating the booking agent. The events planning staff can make recommendations but often senior management makes the final decision.

Advertising & Marketing

A company gala does not need to advertise or market the gala. Some exceptions exist. For example, if the gala is honoring a member of the community the public relations staff will send out releases to all media. Therefore in those cases, events planning and public relations staff need to coordinate.

Importance of Location & Season

For the sake of variety most organizations do not return to the same location year after year unless the gala is actually held on the physical premises of the company. Certain banquet halls, hotels, restaurants that are part of the same parent corporation can provide favorable financial arrangements by holding the gala in one hotel ballroom and a sister company's ballroom the next year. There can be compelling reasons to hold the gala in the same place every year because of some unique characteristic of the location: large size, boat docking capacity, proximity to the organization – but variation is an important factor in making a gala pleasantly memorable.

The events planning staff should rank the characteristic most important in selecting the location for the gala.

- Uniqueness of the venue
- Cost
- Availability of discounts for future events
- Availability at a specific time of the year
- Size of the facility or some part of the facility (i.e., largest ballroom, large lawn for outside event)
- Ease in getting there (i.e., close to major highways, airports, public transportation, expansive parking facilities)

Importance of Date/Time of Year

Galas often have a history and time of the year is part of that history. Galas tend to be scheduled at certain times of the year. May and June are favorite months although winter galas present interesting opportunities for themes. Galas don't want to conflict with other common events so time of the year usually demands steering clear of holidays.

It is recommended that if the date of the gala is not exactly the same each year to check on the Internet and newspapers/magazines for announcements of other events that may present a conflict for prospective attendees. School breaks are one category where families may take their children on vacation including those quasi-winter breaks in February or college spring breaks. Be careful not to conflict with religious holidays (the country is much more diverse than it once was) and the dates of other important organizations' galas.

Chapter 6 Meals

I. Breakfast/Luncheons

Food Choices Are Limited Making the Planning Easier

Special events and food -- the two are inseparable. It is a commonly held principle that food will bring people to an event. However, depending upon tastes and dietary restrictions, any event with food brings its own challenges. The most important issue is cost. The company wants to serve something tasteful, relatively healthy and within budget. To manage or hold down costs the event becomes breakfast or a luncheon rather than dinner.

Many businesses hold monthly meetings as breakfasts or luncheons as a way to satisfy members' or employees' demands for convenience and affordability. If these are routine events – the first Tuesday of the month then the meal choices should at least change with the season of the year. They do not need to be radically different each month but the quality of the food should be decent if not gourmet.

Helpful Hints
• Food and menu alone never make a breakfast or luncheon a success so don't fuss too much

	• If there's a main speaker he/she cannot be dull or boring, no droopy eyes at breakfast
	• Keep the menu light – avoid heavy foods that induce sleepiness
	• Avoid alcohol at lunch – most people go back to work

The breakfast or luncheon usually comes in two varieties – the regularly scheduled meeting and the true special event. The special event breakfast or luncheon usually has a special purpose – honoring someone or another organization, the scholarship award to the deserving high school student or acknowledgement of a special achievement such as a milestone in the organization's history.

Regularly Scheduled Event

Even the regularly scheduled events need some variety to keep them lively and assure regular attendance. Lively can mean alternating among several different restaurants with different menus – different type of cuisine such as Japanese one month, Chinese the next, Italian the following month. If the regularly scheduled meeting follows a specific pattern then something new should be introduced at the meetings such as a guest speaker.

Most membership organizations meet monthly although quarterly or bimonthly are possibilities especially if attendance has been lagging. If winter presents attendance problems then skip January and/or February. Or if summer is a difficult time to gather members skip July and August. A specific restaurant or hotel can provide reasonable prices especially if there's a long history of conducting meetings at this location. However, if attendance is less than desirable change is in order. Good rates are fine but not if people are not showing up for the meetings.

Most membership meetings have a spot for introductions where members and guests introduce themselves and may promote their business or service. To encourage more attendance or more guest attendance attempt something of a more social nature to the meetings such as a raffle or auction. Study some of the proceedings from networking organizations for possible ideas to infuse more energy into these meetings.

Purpose

Regularly scheduled breakfasts or luncheons usually have a long-standing purpose such as the venue for membership meetings. Therefore, the expectations are clear. Here familiarity is important but can be unappealing and counterproductive if the meeting is also designed to attract new members.

An annual breakfast event is unusual but is a highly cost efficient way of honoring an individual or another organization since the meal expenses are low. It is also a highly effective communications method of attracting hard to get professionals to meetings. It is assumed to last no more than ninety minutes and starts earlier than the standard business day sometimes at 6:30 or 7:00 am.

Since an early breakfast event can begin before the normal business day, it is possible to select an unusual venue for the annual occasion such as a museum. Other possible venues to select because of the off-peak nature of breakfast are racetracks (which many now offer gambling and decent dining), flagship department stores many with restaurants or designer shops, and even transportation hubs with dining facilities such as larger Amtrak stations or major commuter transportation centers.

Events can take place in many locations so if it's a group of lawyers perhaps in a distinctive-looking government building, a religious group in an architecturally magnificent house of worship, an arts-based group in an art museum. Think creatively to make an event "feel" special.

Fundraising Event – Corporate Sponsorships

Even a breakfast can be a fundraising event. It's an especially good time of the day for business people and professionals who have no other spare time. Certainly costs are less for food, entertainment is rarely required but sponsors are still essential. Non-profits and community groups do ask for business sponsorships to defray the cost of the meal.

Many hotels offer good venues. The meal itself is not important – any venue can produce an edible breakfast. Hotels and resorts offer convenience.

Closed or Open to the Public

Any event can be closed or open to the public. If there's an important guest speaker it may serve as an excellent way to increase public awareness for both the business sponsor and the non-profit or community group.

Most membership organizations encourage guests at regularly scheduled breakfast meetings but not necessarily the public. How the publicity is conducted should reflect the nature of the organization's openness towards the general public. Guests are brought by members while the public is anyone who learns about the meeting and makes an appearance.

Organizations hoping to increase awareness in the community can invite the press to the breakfast meetings. Often they are provided a complementary meal.

Business Sponsorships Sought

Non-profits and community groups are constantly seeking funding opportunities and, therefore, business sponsorships. What makes a breakfast sponsorship advantageous? Lower costs are a main element. There are other uses for breakfasts.

- Important information can be communicated
- An important local celebrity or guest speaker is readily available in the early mornings
- Inexpensive method of honoring individual or group
- Simple means of celebrating a non-profit or community group's organizational milestone (i.e., organization's anniversary, president's anniversary or retirement)
- Business participates in ribbon cutting or launching of new program (presence of politicians and the press important)
- Local chambers of commerce participate and share expenses for a community breakfast

Honoring Individual/Group

Honorees bring in their own wide web of potential sponsors and supporters. Similar to other honoree events, there is an expectation that the honoree will be an individual or group whose presence results in attracting new people. This can be helpful for a business that participates as a sponsor if this new audience has a potential for becoming new clients for the business.

Honoring people for a condensed period of time such as during breakfast or lunch is less complicated than planning a gala or dinner event. Entertainment is not likely at breakfast, probably not at lunch. The entertainment is speeches about the honoree.

Honorees are anticipating some award. It can be elaborate (i.e., Irish crystal bowl) or simply a plaque. If the event's major purpose is fundraising then a more modest award is a better investment. Depending upon the sponsors, a more elaborate award can be the financial responsibility of a particular sponsor. It is an opportunity to promote a new product or service by the business sponsor.

Importance of Location

A breakfast or lunch event does not require the exacting review that a gala or dinner might entail because of lower expectations. The event is short; the meal is less involved, just one course, coffee and soft drinks. No entertainment and no alcohol decrease costs.

Unlike a gala or dinner event variety is not essential. In fact, convenience may be the most important attribute of the venue. Banquet halls, hotels, restaurants that are sites for galas or dinners or conferences can offer convenience at a reasonable price.

The events planning staff should rank the characteristic most important in selecting the location for the breakfast or luncheon.

- Ease in getting there (i.e., close to major highways, airports, public transportation, expansive parking facilities)
- Uniqueness of the venue (e.g., museum, church, school)
- Cost
- Availability of discounts for future events
- Availability of the time of the year
- Size of the facility or some part of the facility (i.e., largest ballroom, large lawn for outside event)

Educational Component

Any organization that is considering expanding into the educational conference arena can test its capabilities by first organizing a simple breakfast or lunch to serve as an educational meeting. The time consuming difficulty will be obtaining continuing education credits for those attending. Some professions require only a series of two or three hour educational sessions annually to keep current on their licensing or credentialing requirements.

The licensing or credentialing educational organization can recommend the topics to be covered during the educational breakfast/lunch meeting and may even recommend competent instructors.

Marketing Event as means of Marketing Organization – Value to Business Community

A relatively low cost event such as a breakfast or luncheon is an ideal introductory event for the public to learn about an organization or cause. The informality, conciseness and affordability (assuming there's a registration or attendance fee) can result in widespread attendance if the event is marketed and advertised to the appropriate outside audience. It can be an inexpensive way for any business to become associated with a particular non-profit or community group.

The draw is not a meal but what else is going to happen. A guest speaker is an important component. An honoree of great general interest is a plus. Honorees can vary: high school senior scholarship winner, local winning school athletic team or math team, a leading local figure – bank president, minister/rabbi, or an entrepreneur of the year. Factors to consider:

- A speaker who is renown or an expert in a field is a potential draw (assuming s/he volunteers their services)
- The honoree can be a draw especially individuals or teams associated with the local schools
- Promote the speaker or honoree in inexpensive ways thru local cable TV & local radio as well as Internet
- Community organization reaches out to local media for free publicity based on the purpose of the event
- Using the organization's Web site/Facebook page or Twitter account as a prime marketing vehicle starting with "Save the Date" information for the breakfast/luncheon highlighting the speaker or honoree

II. Dinners

What's for dinner?

T here are similarities between any meal as the focus of an event. The differences are of scale and size. People sitting down for dinner are less forgiving about ambiance than breakfast or lunchtime attendees. The possibilities of what to serve is more complex – appetizer, salad, main entrée, dessert versus one item to select. For any business hosting a dinner, the attendees will expect to be wined and dined as well as entertained. Also the business community is constantly being asked to become a sponsor of a non-profit's or community group's major dinner. These are usually annual events. Sometimes there is an honoree. One way non-profits and community groups rope in a business is by honoring a company executive or Board member.

Helpful Hints
• Food variety is required for the menu (meat, fish, chicken, vegetarian)
• For some companies the dinner is the main event of a company gala – lavish and large
• A dinner event draws non-profits and community groups to the business community to serve as sponsors

Purpose

Corporations and businesses of all sizes and industries annually host dinners. Most of these events are tied and directed by the company's sales or marketing divisions. There may also be a charitable purpose if the company has a dedicated charitable giving department or company foundation.

The purpose of the dinner may have a major impact on the amount of money dedicated to the event. Sales events are usually the most lavish. Sometimes they are opportunities for new products or services to be introduced to company associates, industry trade groups or selected members of the public and media. Dinners can also be the places where companies present financial results to a group of financial backers, venture capitalists or bankers. The company's events planning staff will be involved with all these different types of dinners.

There are several purposes for special events dinners:

- Honoring the sales force
- Honoring the business itself because of some important milestone such as historical anniversary, retirement of founder, award received from outside organization
- Raising public awareness of the business or new direction includes special guest speaker or celebrity MC
- Raising public awareness of an issue because of the business's connection to an issue (i.e., new green initiatives, development along a revitalized waterfront, support for some public school projects)

Master- Mistress of Ceremonies

The special dinner event can require a guest or celebrity MC. The factors to consider:

- Traditionally MC hosts this event
- Most important event of the year (no gala)
- Celebrity volunteers to host dinner
- Honoree requests MC

Entertainment Aspects

Depending upon the purpose of the dinner impacts the level and type of entertainment. There may be a need for some minimal entertainment as dinner guests wait to sit at their tables. If there's a cocktail hour before the dinner event then there is an expectation of some type of low key entertainment. It need not be elaborate or expensive – a small classical-style ensemble works or a three-piece jazz group. The size of the entertainment and its complexity is determined as much by the physical layout of the dining area as is the cost.

The special dinner event can require entertainment if there's an expectation of dinner and dancing. The issues to consider:

- Entertainment is historically provided
- Importance of the dinner to company executives, honoree or speaker
- Most important event of the year (no gala)
- Inexpensive local entertainers available

Dining and dancing can mean a twenty-piece orchestra or a college DJ. Reasonably priced entertainment is available to those who search within their communities. As mentioned before, university level music schools (e.g., Curtis Institute of Music in Philadelphia, Oberlin College Conservatory of Music, near Cleveland, Ohio, San Francisco Conservatory of Music, Manhattan School of Music in NYC) offer performing artists to book for events whether it's student performers (classical, contemporary, jazz, opera) or graduates.

Other examples of reasonable or free entertainment are available from an amazing variety of sources in the community (e.g., local choral groups and chorales, children's choruses, musical-style singing groups, community orchestras). Enjoyable entertainment does not have to be expensive.

Closed or Open to the Public

Dinners that have a fundraising component are usually open to the public although the marketing can be selective and tailored to a specific audience. The presence of a guest speaker of renown or an expert in a topic of general interest would support having the event open to the public. In fact, at a special dinner event where there is an important, well-recognized speaker, individual ticket prices can be priced higher even if the speaker is volunteering his/her services.

Sponsorship of Dinners for Non-Profits & Community Groups

A lavish special fundraising dinner event will need sponsors – sponsors – and more sponsors. Companies of all sizes will be asked to contribute. Sponsors buy tables and ads in journal books just as they would be expected to do at a gala. Sponsors can donate and then are expected to buy auction items provided by others in the business community.

Marketing Company New Product

Special event dinners are useful for celebrating the introduction of a new product or service. It can be dinner for the entire staff or those who worked on the project. Or it can be a dinner with selected staff plus appropriate media for maximum public relations value. Or it can be a lavish dinner for financial backers.

71

Equally useful, it can celebrate the success of a new product or service. It's an award to those who contributed to the success of a new product or service. Studies have shown that employees appreciate being thanked and acknowledged for their contributions. It can include a money bonus but it doesn't have to be just money.

Assist Non-Profit or Community Group's Cause

Non-profits and community groups use special event dinners as an opportunity to market a cause or the mission of the non-profit or community group itself. As with most activities involving non-profits or community groups and business, there's money or sponsorships involved. For these type of events the purpose isn't pure fundraising but raising awareness. So the dinner doesn't raise funds but it can't be a money loser so sponsors are still required.

Most of the activities associated with these dinners will be the responsibility of the development staff of the non-profit or community group. Company events planning staff serve as assistants. Perhaps their opinions will be sought by the non-profit or community group staff. Minimally, company staff will work on seating arrangements and any dietary restrictions for company staff or management attending.

Company events planning staff can provide assistance because often the promoting of a non-profit or community group's mission or cause is similar in logistics to marketing a business's new product or service.

- Need to identify the uniqueness or importance of the cause – why people would want to attend the dinner

- Assemble and cultivate an interested local press corps well in advance to announce the forthcoming event
- Increasing awareness is significantly advanced if a local news outlet is one of the sponsors
- Using the organization's Web site, Facebook page or Twitter account as prime marketing vehicles starting with "Save the Date" information about the dinner highlighting its uniqueness

Seating Arrangements

Special event dinners are like galas and seating arrangements are a potential problem unlike more informal meals like breakfasts and lunches. Company sponsors who buy tables should be able to devise their own arrangements.

Chapter 7 Sports Events: Golf or Tennis or Walking Anyone

When Does the Sun Arrive?

Sporting events are extremely popular with organizations of all kinds. Where once this type of event was heavily male-oriented it has since evolved into a much more unisex activity and attracts men and women even children --although it is possible to hold two distinct golfing events (or tennis events) one specifically for men and one for only women. These type of events are popular with employees as stand-alone warm weather events or part of a sales conference. Also businesses of all sizes are eagerly sought out to sponsor sporting events by non-profits and community groups.

Golf Tournament as Fundraising event for non-profits & community groups

Golf is probably the most common non-profit or community group fundraising sports activity but it can be other types such as tennis, yachting/sailing, swimming. It's not only athletes who are enthusiastic about participating in sporting events. Golf, in particular, has been attracting a wider range of players in the last decade.

Typically, businesses will be asked to sponsor some aspect of the tournament. Often if the senior management of the company like to play golf it can be a rewarding, win-win experience. The non-profit or community group benefits from the funds raised by tournament fees and giveaways while the business employees have an enjoyable outing. Company events planning staff may be involved in the planning if their employer has a major fundraising role.

Helpful Hints

- Golf tournaments are the most complicated and difficult event to plan and manage – weather is never predictable

- Consulting firms specializing only in arranging golf tournaments are available to run the event

- Right country club is the draw -- passionate golfers use these as opportunities to golf on courses otherwise unavailable

- Requires insurance

- Contests, contests, contests at least for the 18 holes

- Prizes, trophies, and gifts

- Celebrities matter and sports heroes (current and retired) are important

Selecting Right Golf Course

One of the main attractions for company staff to participate in a golf tournament is the right golf course. Events planning staff arranging for a one-day company golf tournament outing need to find out the best course available in the community. Simple word-of-mouth can be enough. If it's part of a larger sales conference being held at a fashionable resort/hotel complex then one of the reasons for choosing a particular resort can be its renowned golf course. Likewise, a non-profit or community group seeking to raise funds through a golf tournament should be trying to locate the best golf course available. The more exclusive the membership, the more likely outsiders such as company management is willing to pay to play on the course.

The other important draw at a golf tournament is a famous golfer, even a retired one with a large following, participating in the tournament. An additional component of the tournament is a golf clinic, especially, if a recognizable pro is the leading the clinic.

A golf tournament requires determining a timeline and sticking to it. The following is the order of events:

9- 6 Months before Event
- Reviewing and then selecting the course (if part of a sales conference one of the criteria for selecting a particular hotel/resort complex)

Six months before event
- Set the Date and Prepare the Budget
- Produce the materials that will be mailed with registration form and include phone and e-mail addresses, and indicate any dietary restrictions for later meals
- Create a golf Tournament Web page on the company web site
- Get golf course to place a Web page on their Web site.
- Identify potential sport celebrities to golf with other participants and serve as award MC
- Select appropriate golf goodies such as golf shirts, hats, tees, balls, golf gloves and golf bags

- Order golf tournament awards early because of the time required to fulfill orders
- Purchase rain insurance and hole in one insurance

Four months prior to the event
- Prepare food, beverage and liquor order for after the event and include snacks, soft drinks, water to be positioned at various points along the course during the event

30 Days before event
- Prepare registration list and publish on-line and through e-mails registration cut-off date
- Plan on aid stations along the course and make emergency services arrangements with local ambulance company and/or fire department

3 Weeks before
- Prepare goodies bags
- Send confirmation notices via e-mail if possible
- Finalize food/beverages menus
- Prepare golf participant pairings

One week prior to event
- Finalize golf participant pairings
- Finalize all course arrangements
- Confirm celebrities

Days Before
- Meet with course management to review all details
- Create an event day check list that includes persons responsible

Event Day
- All materials delivered to course

- Registration table is set-up
- Set-up contests
- .Inspect food/beverages

Celebrity Involvement

Celebrities at a golf event are usually sports figures not necessarily professional golfers but preferably someone who loves to golf. The celebrity can serve several roles. The most important role is that the celebrity plays golf with participants. It can be one of the biggest draws of the event.

The celebrity beyond playing with the participants can also serve as the host for the after golf dining event. This is also the person who can distribute the awards and serve as a general MC for the event.

Contest Prizes

The complexity of the event is magnified by the need for many prizes. Eighteen holes sometimes mean eighteen different prizes. There is always a hole in one prize. Insurance exists to help cover the risk because the grand prize can be an expensive car or even a golf vacation costing thousands of dollars. The more players the more expensive is the insurance.

Entertainment Aspects

Entertainment is usually not necessary for this type of event unless the participants are bringing along non-players. This happens when the after tournament dining is seen as an event unto itself. Also, some golf events permit children as non-players and then entertainment should be child-oriented. The golf event can include a golf clinic for children before the tournament event. The course's golf pro can be in charge.

Walkathons and other "a-thons"

When is it going to rain?

In this age of fitness and with concerns about health issues such as diabetes and heart disease, the value of a walkathon or bike-a-thon has vast appeal to company employees. A company can become the sponsor of a non-profit or community group's event. It is one that can involve the greater community so it's an opportunity to engage with the community, to promote a healthy image of the company.

What makes this event popular is that it is something that can include everyone – young, old, healthy and those in wheelchairs. This is an outside event and so all event organizers are ultimately at the mercy of the elements. One schedules these events for the best possible type of weather – not too cold, not hot, sunny and warm but not dehydrating, absent of too much wind, rain, ice or sleet. So like marathons the usual months selected are not in the heat of the summertime; the best months are May, September or early October.

Helpful Hints
• Early planning required to obtain city permits for walking in the streets, health permits for food vendors
• Every entry needs a concession gift -- tee shirt, hat

	• Find a celebrity host associated with healthy lifestyles

Logistical Issues for Company Events Planners

The uniqueness of the walkathon as a special event revolves around the issue of creating teams of participants who will pay the registration fees and join the event or simply make a contribution with no intention of participating. Each team has a leader who finds these individuals. Event organizers have limited control about whom and how participants are recruited. It is a highly diffuse event with much of the control dispersed among tens of volunteers. For company evens planners, teaming up with a non-profit or community group to participate simplifies some of the logistical headaches associated with walkathons.

Registration Materials

Walkathons are recognized special events so there's no need to reinvent the wheel. Borrow from other walkathons' registration materials. Use the Internet as an excellent reference guide.

Typically, several types of forms are required:

- Multi-purpose Registration Form check off - boxes for registration fee and donations and tee-shirt size
- Liability Waiver Information (can be included on the registration form)
- Donation Form for those not participating in walkathon
- Pledge/Donation Form
- Team Information sheet

Celebrity Involvement

There are several ways to view the use of a celebrity for a walkathon. They can be a big draw that attracts people who typically wouldn't walk. Many participants in events including celebrities are usually touched in some personal way with the cause or the issue as the result of some problem/tragedy affecting family members or themselves.

The role of a celebrity is to encourage people to attend. This happens in two ways. First, the celebrity uses their own promotional resources to promote the event. They speak to the press about the event. In addition, on the day of the event the celebrity hands out all the prizes. The celebrity if he/she donates their time should receive a gift.

/Business Participation as a Sponsor

Every event needs key sponsors. For a walkathon business sponsors are needed for at least the following items:

- Food and refreshments
- Insurance costs
- Awards
- Registration gifts such as tee shirts/hats

Entertainment Aspects

Children often are involved in these events. But their presence may require some type of child-oriented entertainment such as a clown or juggler. Entertainment can be as simple as loud speakers for amplification provided by a local radio station.

A nice touch is arranging with a local high school band or other community musical group to play at the start of the walkathon and as part of the award ceremony. School groups are frequently available.

Awards/Gifts

All participants receive some kind of gift such as a tee shirt or hat or water bottle with the event name and date as well as the names of any event sponsors. To promote fitness and healthy lifestyles all food and refreshments should be healthily and nutritious. In addition, if any gift bags are distributed they should include educational materials.

Chapter 8 Excursions: Jaunts Here and There

Al communities present opportunities to reward staff or contribute donations to worthwhile charities by providing enjoyable jaunts to the sporting arena, art museum, zoo or the theater. These planned events can also be used as morale boosters for employees. And they can be planned as annual special events or more frequently since tickets are always available.

Sports Outings
Batter Up

Add something different to the mix of employee benefits Sports outings are extremely popular with a wide range of different audiences, young and old, men and women. They are easy to arrange and most college and professional sports teams can easily accommodate groups of 20 or more through the sport team's group sales office. An additional activity is a tour of the stadium, meet and greet the players. These are not usually the team stars but there are still opportunities to obtain signed autographs. Major league teams have more elaborate arrangements such as visiting the dugout, participants high five the players as they enter the field, refreshments with the players, lunch at the players club. These are all activities that can be arranged with the team's group sales office. Availability is always dependent upon the team's popularity.

Sports outings are excellent and easy to arrange as donations to area charities or as rewards to local school athletes or winning chess team. Sports is yearlong – baseball in spring and summer, hockey in fall and winter, basketball in winter and spring, football in fall and winter. Pick a sport and there's an available team. Practically every community has some kind of sporting team nearby.

- Minor and major league baseball
- College baseball
- Minor and major league hockey
- College hockey
- College lacrosse
- College and professional soccer
- College basketball
- Professional basketball

If the community is located by a college there's also likely to be low-key sporting events or important meets that can become employee rewards. Even smaller colleges have competitive sports teams that participate in NCAA and NAIA tournaments. This can be college track and field, swimming, field hockey, tennis, volleyball. Opportunities exist.

Begin with contacting several teams' group sales office. Some teams may offer better packages. Often this is determined by how well the team is doing competitively that year and the number of unsold tickets available. Also the company can leverage its group sales with obtaining additional items such as signed autographed photos of individual players and/or the team, tickets, tours of the playing field, which can be used as part of the sporting event package or later for a sales/marketing gala or major dinner event.

Helpful Hints

	• Easy and fun, the whole family can be involved
	• Every major and minor and college team offer packages
	• Create a day-long event by renting a bus for the group
	• Giveaway tickets to employees or as contributions to local charities for them to giveaway

Theater Outings

Comedy – Drama -- Musical

Want to try something different? Theatrical events are one proven pleaser just avoid the controversial. Of course, there is the grandest theatrical center in the country in New York City. But most major cities in the US operate important regional non-profit theatres as well as commercial theaters in cities such as Chicago, Boston, Los Angeles, Houston, Minneapolis, Washington D.C., Atlanta.

In addition, colleges and universities operate theater programs, which present plays, musicals, and opera to the public. In fact, these college programs are hungry for greater public recognition. There are some terrific college programs in the country. Any college or university that offers degrees in theater or classical vocal programs is going to offer public performances during the course of the school year. More than fifty (50) colleges and universities offer theater programs. Also, there are community theater groups, which can be commercial or non-profit that present plays and musicals. All of these groups have the ability to help you create a theatrical outing as an employee reward or as a giveaway to area charities to use as a fundraiser.

Similar to sports teams the place to begin discussions is with the group sales office. Smaller community theatre groups may not have a distinct group sales office but the box office manager can be accommodating.

In the opera world, there have been some new developments that can become important either as employee rewards or contributions to area charities to use as fundraising events. The Metropolitan Opera (Met) in New York City has made arrangements with certain select movie theaters across the country to broadcast live opera performances. These performances have proved to be very popular. The Met is planning on expanding its offerings in the coming seasons. The Met's success will undoubtedly be copied by other opera companies seeking new audiences. This has spread to ballet companies and European theater groups. Events planning staff should keep abreast of these developments. It makes the company seem cutting edge and concerned about their employees as well as using these events as giveaways to benefit charities.

Helpful Hints
• Easy and fun to plan; can evolve into a regular event (quarterly, semi-annually, annually)
• Offer the widest range of variety (drama, comedy, musicals, opera, ballet)
• Create a day-long event by renting a bus for the group, providing lunch or dinner
• Giveaway tickets to employees or as

	contributions to local charities for them to giveaway

Also, a company can use these events to raise awareness of an issue in the community. For example, a company can lend its name to a local organization dedicated to providing transitional housing for battered women and children by purchasing tickets and donating those tickets to a theatrical outing about the subject. The event can be both educational and entertaining. Check the advance schedules of commercial, local community theaters and college theater departments. Be aware that theatrical openings are notoriously unreliable and delays are common. If this is a first attempt and it's important for the event to run smoothly select a show in the middle of its designated run.

Other Types of Outings

Culture at Christmas or take the grandchildren to the Zoo

Museums, zoos and botanical gardens offer group packages. At holiday times, many museums offer specific exhibitions with a holiday theme. Seasonal exhibitions are common at botanical gardens. All of these are more opportunities to provide first class cultural entertainment to reward employees or as giveaways to local charities. Contact your museums, zoos or botanical gardens.

Chapter 9 Groundbreakings & Ribbon Cuttings: *Meet and Greet with Local Dignitaries*

Politicians Love To Attend Especially around Election Cycles

R ibbon cuttings have been a normal part of business for a hundred years since the early part of the last century. Typically, the company ties a ceremonial ribbon at the entrance and the scissors used for the ribbon cutting are kept as souvenirs. Local dignitaries were always part of the event forcing participants to listen to verbose politicians.

And the idea still lives. Think free publicity and public relations. The event does not have to be large to be effective as a means of getting the company positive public recognition. They are also short events lasting no longer than two hours with most of the ceremony completed in 30 minutes. They should also be held during normal business hours 9:00 AM to 4:30 PM and not on Fridays or too close to holidays. Politicians around election time have tight schedules.

Typical schedule:

- Arrival of Guests
- Mingle/Networking
- Brief Speech by Company Representative (the more senior the better)

- Recognition of special guests (i.e., politicians, clergy)
- Pictures (company's photographer or one hired for the event)
- Actual Ribbon Cutting
- Refreshments, tours of the new facility and more networking (lasting no more than an hour)

Helpful Hints
• Make certain to get on the politician's calendar as soon as possible
• During an election year politicians are most likely to attend
• Publicity is essential   contact all media outlets
• Substitute free publicity for advertising

All ribbon cuttings and groundbreaking ceremonies should be treated as events, which mean that a press release is sent out about 30 days in advance. Formal invitations to high ranking local officials need to be sent via regular mail. All others should receive e-mail announcements. A reminder is often necessary. Always request a RSVP so you have a good idea of attendance for ordering refreshments. You can include a map if the location is not easy to find or it's a new location.

All companies should know their local politicians – state legislature, local city hall, US Congress. Make ample opportunities for those politicians to know the products and services available through the company, and the names of key staff members perhaps even the names of members of the Board of Directors.

Invite local legislative staff to all events and create events just for them such as a tour of the company's facility or a luncheon with a select group of company staff. These are valuable people and certainly should be on the company's important contact list. These types of events require an actual ceremonial scissor, ribbons, markers and a photographer.

Many companies find it very useful to be members of the local Chamber of Commerce. The values of membership need to be weighed against the costs. However, if the company belongs to a local Chamber of Commerce, call upon Chamber staff because they are available to help in the planning and publicity of events such as ribbon cuttings. In many cases, the local Chamber has a ceremonial scissor to borrow and the membership will attend if added attendance would be helpful. Chambers of Commerce view this type of event as vital to their own mission.

Chapter 10 Employee-Centered Events: *Keep the Troops Satisfied*

Traditionally, employers have sponsored annual employee-oriented events. It could be the picnic in the summer or the holiday party at the end of the year. There are also work anniversary dinners for achieving employment milestones such as ten and/or twenty-five years.

Employees Party on Employer's Expense

Employee Appreciation Day

This is a recognized business holiday, which aims to provide an opportunity for employers to thank their staffs. The history of Employee Appreciation Day is murky but is thought to be an outgrowth of the establishment in 1958 with the U.S. Chamber of Commerce of Boss's Day. Although Employee Appreciation Day is recognized as the first Friday in March, in fact, employers can hold events at times most convenient to the company and their employees. Many events are held during the warm months and include employees' families.

Typically, the events planning staff would work with an Employee Committee since the whole idea is to do things appreciated by the employees and not senior management. If the company is unionized then the highest ranking union representatives would be the place to start with organizing the committee. The events planning staff can also encourage committee membership through an open invitation process publicized on the company's intranet. Usually, this is a full-day event and all employees are encouraged to participate while operations are either closed or are handled by a skeleton staff of volunteers, who will be given leave at another time.

The first important decision is whether to include the families of employees. The second issue is this entirely cost-free to the employee or does the company subsidize the costs or are guests charged a fee. Management can make those determinations although soliciting employees' attitudes about bringing the family is useful. Obviously, it will be far more costly to host an event that includes spouses, significant others and children. Since this is a day dedicated to appreciating the employees it's important to elicit ideas from the staff about the day's activities.

An intranet survey is probably one efficient way of learning the following:

- Supportive of bringing the family even if guests are charged a fee
- Picking a day for the event (provide 2-3 choices)
- Ideas about what they want to do on that day
- Possible location
- Type of Entertainment (influenced whether families and children are invited)

The events planning staff working with a management approved budget can determine the refreshments. Normally, at least a lunch of some type is provided and there should also be snacks available during the day. Another important consideration is whether each guest receives a gift of some type.

The events planning staff may also be involved with planning the activities of the day. The venue selected will determine some of the activities. Possible venues include:

- Company location (headquarters or some other facility)
- Hotel or Resort (summer availability of golf, tennis, swimming is highly regarded)
- Day camps or sleep-away camps (many are eager to rent their facilities off-season – good month is June or mid-September)
- Local college with expansive athletic facilities and dining available during college vacation periods (spring break, holidays)
- Local movie theater during off-hours providing movie or other entertainment as well as popcorn and hotdogs
- Trip to area amusement park includes admission and a package with food and rides
- State or county fair with admission and food package
- Sporting or theatrical event (see previous chapter)

If games or contests are part of the day's events then there's an expectation of prizes. The events staff may be requested to buy them.

If the company embarks on this type of event then be certain that the emphasis is on pleasing the employee and not satisfying management. A poorly executed plan for an Employee Appreciation Day can have serious negative consequences. The objective is to boost morale and thank employees. You don't want employees leaving and thinking anything else.

Company Volunteer Day

Americans volunteer. According to the government, more than a quarter of all Americans volunteered once last year. That's more than 60 million people. The picture of the most likely volunteer is:

- Female
- Between 35-44 years of age
- Married people with children under 18
- Well educated with the highest percentage among college graduates
- Spent a median of 52 hours during the year volunteering
- Women performed fundraising activities, tutor/teach, collect/distribute/prepare/serve food
- Men performed general labor, coaching, providing professional/managerial assistance

At a time when finances are tight, a company sponsored day of volunteering is a great morale booster and potentially a free day of labor for area charities. It is said that people receive great satisfaction by volunteering. A non-profit can work with a company's human resources department to arrange a Day of Volunteering.

Working with the human resources department of the non-profit or community group, the company events planning staff needs to learn what type of volunteers they need. Usually, the local charity will offer more than one project. Let someone in human resources determine whether they want to offer their employees choices. Also have the local charity clearly communicate the amount of time for this commitment. Company events planning staff should not assume the local charity needs these volunteers for a 7-8 hour day unless you ask.

Examples of company volunteer projects include:

- Assisting an organization such as Habitat for Humanity building a house or a major renovation
- Planting a community garden
- Planting trees in a community park
- Painting or low-level maintenance at a non-profit's offices
- Trail maintenance for an environmental group
- Environmental clean-up of parks, rivers, coastal areas
- Meals served at community agencies for the homeless, victims of domestic violence, veteran's groups
- Tutoring for low-income children

Successful Volunteer Days can lead to community benefits and can include:

- More personal volunteering by company participants
- Individual donations by company participants
- Company contribution
- Further involvement by company in future fundraising events such as galas, dinners, walkathons
- Organization's addition to the company's charitable giving list
- Grant award by corporation that has a charitable foundation

Chapter 11 Other Types of Events

"Taste Of" – Food Events

How good is the food?

A common summertime event is the annual "Taste Of" event. It is usually a method to increase community awareness of the different hometown restaurants and other small businesses. Larger-size company involvement is usually limited unless it's to raise the company's image or presence in the community. In this case, company events planning staff needs to work with the organizing group.

Usually, the organizing group is either a local chamber of commerce, "Main Street" non-profit or downtown business association. A local fraternal organization can also be involved or sponsor the event– Rotary, Elks, Lions or Kiwanis.

It is the type of event that requires the cooperation of local officials and often town permits, if it is held in a public place. Typically, these events close off vehicular traffic in a downtown area. Each town and city has its own particular bureaucracy and some places are more adept at processing these legal requirements. If this is a first time event or under consideration, carefully explore how quickly and easily these things can be processed in developing the event timeline.

However, a "Taste Of" event doesn't have to be held in the streets of a town. It can be located at a school playing field with proper protection of the grass and grounds. A large banquet house during an off-peak season can physically host a "Taste Of" event.

Town Event – Special Permits

A "Taste Of" event that closes public streets or involves the sale of food requires government permits. The first requirement is to find out which town or village agency handles the type of permit(s) that will be required to hold a "Taste Of" event. The town may also require additional fiduciary documentation such as surety bonds and/or insurance. The event may also require additional expenses to pay for off-duty police and/or fire personnel at the event or readily available. Company involvement can include donations to off-set these ancillary expenses.

Helpful Hints
• Weather is the enemy although there is rain insurance
• Late spring, summer, and early fall are the best weather choices although Winter-holiday oriented "Taste Of" events can be highly successful
• Closing the streets requires town permits and government bureaucracy
• Collaborative events with local Chambers of Commerce and/or local fraternal organizations

One needs to consider how to structure the finances of holding such an event. There are several possibilities. Each vendor can pay the exact same fee. There can be a sliding scale based on criteria: size of booth, size of company, willingness to share in some other event expenses. Different type of vendors pay different fees – local restaurants pay less and media companies pay more. Chamber of Commerce members pay less and others pay more.

Involvement of Politicians

During election year cycles local/state politicians love to be seen at these types of events. Although it's important for this type of event to be viewed as non-political. The mayor, town supervisor, selectmen may want to be involved as speakers, ribbon cutters and their presence needs to be incorporated into the planning process. However, the presence of local politicians is more likely to assure media attention and that can be very helpful to the event.

Entertainment Aspects

This is the fun and memorable part of the event. But it also involves more work to select the most audience-friendly entertainment within budget. These are family-oriented events and so jugglers and clowns are appreciated for the young ones. If there's physical space and the ability to set-up an outdoor theater for child-oriented entertainment such as puppet shows or a magician do so. It's a great draw since children are often bored by sampling food.

A key adult attraction is musical bands. The entertainment can be simple. Hire one local band, which plays all day in the same location on a portable stage. Normally, this is a designated area where beer can be sold. It can have tables and chairs and sheltered by a tent. It can also serve as the dining area.

Awards

This can be tricky. The expectation is that there are awards of some kind. The press likes to report on winners. So how do you select award winners without creating hurt feelings or fallout? A survey is created and every restaurant is listed. Most probably, people taste some but not all the food vendors and check a box. Event organizers collect the surveys and tabulate the results at the end of the event. Then the results are announced. Or the local media can design, collect, tabulate and announce the winners. So the results may not be immediate but appear in the local newspaper, on the radio or TV following the event.

An alternative approach is to create an award food tasting panel. These would be individuals not directly linked to any one restaurant or food establishment. If there's a culinary school nearby or a food service program in the local high school, the teachers and students can serve as the tasting panel.

Chapter 12 Start Your Own Events Planning Business: *I Want to Be My Own Boss*

Y ou have been working as the events planner for a non-profit, hotel/resort, private company, but you want more flexibility and the ability to better utilize your growing skill sets. Starting your own events planning business is the next giant step. Then similar to any small business, it's important to develop that business plan and consult the local office of the Small Business Administration (SBA) for free seminars and advice. Some of that information is available on-line. If financing is an issue the SBA is also a great source for information on loans including government guaranteed ones.

Networking and marketing the business are essential as is setting up a Web site. Contact vendors who once came to you for business and ask them for a reciprocal favor. This type of business is all about who you know and people putting out a good word about you and your expertise. Join organizations and meet people at every opportunity.

Social versus organization events planning

Pick a specific market for your business. Social events planning refers to working with individuals and families for such events as weddings, birthdays, anniversaries, graduation parties, children's parties, retirement parties. This is a steady market. Some planners become highly specialized and only deal in weddings because of its potential complexities and large budgets. The entire social events planning business is a market open to imaginative ideas but one dictated by the whims of individuals who may have their own ideas. It can be difficult to manage big egos but there are many more individuals and families seeking advice than corporations or non-profits. Busy people need help in making the arrangements.

Organization events planning refers to corporations, business associations, convention centers, non-profits. While non-profits arrange events for multi-purposes many are geared towards fundraising. Corporations develop events tied to sales conferences, marketing activities, public relations. The burden of constantly finding ways of raising money is absent from corporations and the budgets tend to be more generous. All large corporations maintain conference planning and events planning staffs. However, in the age of efficiency many more firms are interested in outsourcing these activities.

Credentials

People who are going to spend lavishly on an event want some demonstrative proof of one's abilities to plan a great event. One simple way is through educational credentials. If you don't already have a certificate or degree in events planning management consider getting one from an area college before launching the new business. It is the most cost efficient use of your own resources and most local public community colleges are affordable.

Start-up Expenses

One can start this type of business on a shoestring from one's own home using lots of temporary help. They don't have to be permanent employees. The usual start-up business expenses include the following categories:

- Rent or carve out a home office
- Equipment (i.e., purchase computer, office furniture, copier, while event equipment is usually rented i.e., tents, chairs, tables, etc.)
- Office Supplies (i.e., stationery, printer toner)
- Web site
- Inventory (samples to use for illustrative purposes)
- Licenses and taxes
- Phones, Fax lines
- Fees for professional association memberships
- Payroll (temporary and/or permanent)
- Advertising/Promotion (e.g., business cards, brochures, advertising)
- Legal Fees & Accounting
- Insurance
- Events software to track expenses

Choosing vendors

Nothing is more career crushing for an events planner then contracting with unreliable or shoddy vendors. One of the most important starting activities is finding good vendors. And depending on your target audience you will need a list of vendors for everything from tableware rentals to floor stage, flowers, food, lighting, entertainment. If your business is more likely to be concentrated at certain popular times of the year for events (i.e., weddings in June, school graduations in May) than find several vendors for every item.

What to Ask Prospective Clients

The key requirement for a successful events planner is listening. The events planner is not a dictator telling the client what to do but listens and creates a vision for the client based on information they give you. At a first meeting with a prospective client making a great first impression is crucial, especially, if the business is new.

- Be punctual for all appointments including telephone appointments
- Be exceptionally well organized
- Be active and convey a sense of urgency because events planning requires energy and motivation

Start an interview with a prospective client by asking simple open-ended questions. Avoid closed questions because you want the prospective client to brainstorm with you. Use open-ended words such as:

- How
- Who
- What
- When
- Where
- Why

And avoid starting questions with closed-end words such as can you, could you, would you, do you. Not all clients have a clear idea about what they want or expect from the event. It's the job of the events planner to find out what they want and what they can afford.

The starting point is of course the purpose of the event. The events planner is the one designing the theme to match the purpose. The prospective client should know about a potential date or at least month of the year, and which year. Then it's the basics of how many people and the budget. One way for prospective clients to understand the finances of an event is to ask about their price per person range.

Questions prospective clients will ask

You can expect to be questioned by the prospective client. Possible client questions include:

- How long have you been planning events? (presumably new business owners have experience as former employees)
- Training (degree or certification may matter)
- References
- Which vendors do you use?
- Do you accept commissions or professional discounts from any vendors you refer?
- Will you be attending meetings with the venue staff, caterers, florists, other vendors?
- Will you review all contracts?
- Who signs the contracts?
- Do we pay each vendor or do we pay you and then you take care of all these individual payments?
- When will you arrive and leave on the day of the event?
- How many other of your planning staff will be at the event?
- Are these employees or temps?
- Do you have any other events scheduled for that same day?
- What's the backup plan? (i.e., inclement weather for an outdoor event, vendor fails to arrive, you get sick, etc.)
- How do you deal with crises – give an example of an event that could have been a failure but was saved by you?
- Do you have insurance?
- What's the fee structure? (e.g., hourly fees, flat fees, percentage)
- Do you charge for an initial consultation and if so can the fee be applied to your final charges if you are hired for the job?

- What is your cancellation policy?

Writing the Events Proposal

The first step is to interview the prospective client to find out about the event and the preliminary budget. In the early discussions recognize immediately if the client's expectations can be matched by the proposed budget. Clients may not understand or be familiar with costs for decorations, linens, entertainment. You should charge a prospective client for a proposal. The consultation fee can be small $150-250, (indicates commitment to actually moving forward with the event). The amount can be applied towards the event for those selecting you. Make this clear to the prospective client upfront so they know not to waste their time or your time.

The proposal should consider contingencies. Some costs rise even during a short period of time. And there's also the possibility that a particular item may become unavailable. All events proposals should include sketches or photographs, which can be linked to your Web site or the Web site of your vendors. Events planning firms often fail because they do not know how to price the event and do not leave enough margin for profit. Do not cheat yourself.

Typically, a proposal will consist of four elements :

- Cover Letter
- Title Page for the Event
- Services to be Provided
- Company History

Clearly, the largest part of the proposal is the services provided with a compelling message in the cover letter about what are the benefits to the prospective client for doing business with you, the events planner. A new business will not have much history but even if it's the first proposal, the events planner has experience and perhaps credentials. You must provide references so use an organization or people from a former employer if this is your first proposal. Ideally, you can solicit references from these people as you are leaving your employer to start your new business venture.

Services provided by an events planner for a full-scale event include:

- Consulting & Planning for the event (e.g., venue choices, theme ideas)
- Accommodations (i.e., at venue location if it's a hotel, Bed & Breakfast, camp grounds)
- Transportation (e.g., limo services, cabs, rental cars)
- Dining & Beverage choices (e.g., menu, premium brands vs. house brands, wine/beer vs. liquor, open bar)
- Decorations (flowers, balloons, candles)
- Rentals (tables/chairs, dinnerware/silverware, linens, dance floor, tents)
- Set-Up
- Music & entertainment (hiring band, DJ, string quartet)
- Recommend vendors for invitations (design, printing and mailing), publicity
- Break-down & Clean-up

Pricing

Always require a deposit with any signed contract with a client. There are several pricing structures depending upon the size of the event.

- Percentage of total costs (10-15%)
- Flat fee
- By the hour

Variations can include fee for the events planner plus a percentage of the vendor fees (i.e., music, decorations, food/beverages). The planner buys flowers from a florist and marks them up 15 percent and charges that amount to the client. Some clients want to use their own vendors for decorations or catering but if you're involved in the selection process you want to be compensated.

How to Get Started

You can produce beautiful business cards and brochures. The Web site can spark. Placing ads in local newspapers or on the Internet is another possibility.

The most impressive way to jumpstart an events planning business is to host an event. Begin by throwing a party celebrating the launching of your events planning business. Invite your target market whether its individuals and families or area organizations. It's imperative that the event is well organized and runs smoothly. Follow-up with all your attendees and solicit their opinions about your event.

Chapter 13 Conclusion

Events planning is an exciting and rewarding occupation. Opportunities are expected to increase over the next decade. Employers are many and represent a variety of industries and businesses including non-profits and government.

Education has become an increasingly important requirement for special events planners. The options are varied: Masters degree, baccalaureate degree, associate degree and shorter certificate programs. Courses and degrees are available across the country in both public and private schools.

A successful events planner requires a certain kind of personality. It is not the career for everybody. Specific personal characteristics are necessary:

- Multi-tasker – more tasks to be completed than hours in a day
- Highly Organized – logistics demands absolute attention to details
- Capable of working under stress
- Flexibility – things always go wrong
- Ability to stay perky and peppy through long hours – events stretch from morning to midnight and sometimes for days on end

This book was developed to provide a concise review of the events planning field. It was designed to assist the novice, the experienced planner and those considering the career. It provided a broad spectrum of information that was helpful for most aspects of events planning. Events covered in the book included:

- Conference
- Gala
- Dining Experiences – breakfast, lunch and dinner
- Sporting Events
- Sports and Theater Outings
- Ground Breakings & Ribbon Cuttings
- "Taste Of" food events
- Employee-Centered Events

The book also provided a simple primer on starting your own events planning business. For the adventurer seeking control over their business life, the chance of becoming an entrepreneur should always be considered. It doesn't take a great deal of start-up funds. It required experience and the willingness to take risk.

Career Tips

If you're uncertain about how well this career fits with your lifestyle and interests then consider simple introductions to the events planning business. For example, students should search out internship opportunities. This can be a good basic introduction to the career without a major commitment. If the internship experience is exciting and makes a positive impression then consider completing a degree or certificate program concentrating on events planning.

Gain experience as a volunteer. There are undoubtedly many organizations in your community that host events. If you are most impressed by a particular non-profit or community group then seek out the events planning staff and inquire about volunteer opportunities.

OTHER TITLES FROM OCEAN BREEZE PRESS

NON-FICTION

"Special Events Planning for Non-Profits"
by Harriet Grayson– complement to this book

"Guide to Grants Writing for Non-Profits" by Harriet Grayson

"Guide to Government Grants & Vendor Opportunities" by Harriet Grayson

Order   now: www.5starseminars.net

FICTION

Sasha Perlov Mystery Series by Anastasia Goodman

"Loose Ends" the first in the Sasha Perlov Series

"Terror in Brooklyn" continues the exploits of police detective Sasha Perlov

Soon to be released "Death and Diamonds"
Novels combine history, mystery & current events.

Order:
www.anastasiagoodman.weebly.com

Like Sasha's Facebook Page
www.facebook.com/sashaperlovdetective

All titles also available in soft cover & Kindle versions

Order: www.amazon.com